Salt Essentials

Craig Sebenik and Thomas Hatch

Beijing · Boston · Farnham · Sebastopol · Tokyo

Salt Essentials

by Craig Sebenik and Thomas Hatch

Printed in the United States of America.

Published by O'Reilly Media, Inc., 1005 Gravenstein Highway North, Sebastopol, CA 95472.

O'Reilly books may be purchased for educational, business, or sales promotional use. Online editions are also available for most titles (*http://safaribooksonline.com*). For more information, contact our corporate/institutional sales department: 800-998-9938 or *corporate@oreilly.com*.

Editors: Courtney Nash and Brian Anderson
Production Editor: Matthew Hacker
Copyeditor: Rachel Monaghan
Proofreader: Sonia Saruba

Indexer: Judith McConville
Interior Designer: David Futato
Cover Designer: Ellie Volckhausen
Illustrator: Rebecca Demarest

June 2015:   First Edition

Revision History for the First Edition
2015-06-05:   First Release

See *http://oreilly.com/catalog/errata.csp?isbn=9781491900635* for release details.

978-1-491-90063-5

[LSI]

Table of Contents

Preface

Who Should Read This Book

Do you want to automate your infrastructure? What about managing your configuration files? Do you use Python? Salt provides a system to manage simple and complex infrastructures. This book will give you an introduction if you have never used Salt, touching on the major pieces and giving you enough information to feel comfortable in deploying Salt in a major production infrastructure.

Whether you are a sysadmin responsible for the installation and maintenance of the operating system or you are a devops engineer at a startup responsible for getting your code to hundred of systems, Salt is a tool to make your job easier. Salt is used by small and large companies to manage tasks ranging from maintaining the basic operating system parameters and configuration all the way to deploying and configuring custom applications.

Many of the examples in this book assume that you have some basic familiarity with Python and YAML. But knowledge of these technologies is not an absolute requirement. If you have some programming experience and some experience with basic data formats (e.g., JSON or XML), then you should be able to follow along without much trouble. At an even more basic level, you should have some working knowledge of Linux and a basic filesystem layout.

Salt can help you solve a wide variety of problems. One of its best features is that, as with Python, much of Salt's internals are exposed to you. This book only gives a glimpse into the possibilities of working with Salt, but it will provide you with a basic understanding from which you can dive into more of the details independently.

Why We Wrote This Book

When I (Craig) first started learning Salt, I was overwhelmed by its features, terms, and even some of the concepts. The more I worked with it and the more I learned, the more I wanted to use Salt to solve even more problems. As Salt spread in my company, I saw my coworkers struggle the same way I did. The documentation on the SaltStack website is great, but it wasn't sufficient. I wrote this book because I wanted others to be able to jump right in with a solid understanding of the basics.

What This Book Is Not

Salt is a great tool for solving a large and various set of problems. Salt grows more and more every day. Mew features are added, existing features are improved, and unnecessary or outdated code is removed. I wanted to give a firm base from which you could learn more and more about Salt. But, covering everything Salt can do is well beyond the scope of a single book. Our goal is to cover the basics, the essentials of Salt. This book will give you a solid platform to build upon. The topics in this book are generally considered to be the most heavily used features of Salt. But the coverage is far from complete. This is a great place to start, but not the only place to learn about Salt.

Once you have the basics down, the documentation on the SaltStack website (*http://docs.saltstack.com/en/latest/*) is a great place to learn more, including details on plenty of advanced features that are, unfortunately, beyond the scope of this book.

A Word on Salt Today

Salt has a very large and heavily engaged user base. It is one of the most contributed projects on GitHub. SaltStack is the company behind Salt. It offers services and training for Salt itself, and is fully committed to Salt being *open core*. There is an active mailing list, a very chatty IRC channel, and plenty of discussions and pull requests on GitHub. As of this writing, version 2015.2.0 (codenamed *Lithium*) was released.

Navigating This Book

This book is organized roughly as follows:

- Chapter 1 introduces the basic organization of Salt.
- Chapter 2 gives a quick summary of the basic command-line utilities.
- Chapters 3 and 4 introduce you to two of the fundamental pieces of Salt: the remote execution engine and the state system.
- Chapter 5 guides you through the basic data elements at the core of Salt.
- Chapters 6 and 8 describe how you can extend and customize Salt.
- Chapters 7 and 9 give more information on the main control point (the Salt master) and some various ways you can structure Salt.

- The final chapter, Chapter 10, gives a very simple introduction to using Salt in a cloud infrastructure.

If you have used Salt even a little, you can likely skip Chapters 1 through 3 and give 4 a quick skim. If you are only interested in customizing the core of Salt, then Chapters 6 and 8 would be of the most interest. However, it is important to note that the examples do build on one another. So, using the examples in, say, Chapter 4, does depend on you having gone through the examples in Chapters 2 and 3. The companion code (*https://github.com/craig5/salt-essentials-utils*) should be able to fill in the gaps.

Online Resources

The Salt documentation (*http://docs.saltstack.com/en/latest/*) is very thorough and a fantastic reference. The documentation pages will link to all of the resources you need to learn even more about Salt and the various technologies used.

Conventions Used in This Book

The following typographical conventions are used in this book:

Italic
: Indicates new terms, URLs, email addresses, filenames, and file extensions.

`Constant width`
: Used for program listings, as well as within paragraphs to refer to program elements such as variable or function names, databases, data types, environment variables, statements, and keywords.

`Constant width bold`
: Shows commands or other text that should be typed literally by the user.

`Constant width italic`
: Shows text that should be replaced with user-supplied values or by values determined by context.

This icon signifies a tip or suggestion.

This element signifies a general note.

This icon indicates a warning or caution.

Using Code Examples

Supplemental material (code examples, exercises, etc.) is available for download at *https://github.com/craig5/salt-essentials-utils.*

This book is here to help you get your job done. In general, if example code is offered with this book, you may use it in your programs and documentation. You do not need to contact us for permission unless you're reproducing a significant portion of the code. For example, writing a program that uses several chunks of code from this book does not require permission. Selling or distributing a CD-ROM of examples from O'Reilly books does require permission. Answering a question by citing this book and quoting example code does not require permission. Incorporating a significant amount of example code from this book into your product's documentation does require permission.

We appreciate, but do not require, attribution. An attribution usually includes the title, author, publisher, and ISBN. For example: "*Salt Essentials* by Craig Sebenik and Thomas Hatch (O'Reilly). Copyright 2015 Craig Sebenik and Thomas Hatch, 978-1-491-90063-5."

If you feel your use of code examples falls outside fair use or the permission given above, feel free to contact us at *permissions@oreilly.com.*

Safari® Books Online

 *Safari Books Online* is an on-demand digital library that delivers expert content in both book and video form from the world's leading authors in technology and business.

Technology professionals, software developers, web designers, and business and creative professionals use Safari Books Online as their primary resource for research, problem solving, learning, and certification training.

Safari Books Online offers a range of plans and pricing for enterprise, government, education, and individuals.

Members have access to thousands of books, training videos, and prepublication manuscripts in one fully searchable database from publishers like O'Reilly Media, Prentice Hall Professional, Addison-Wesley Professional, Microsoft Press, Sams, Que,

Peachpit Press, Focal Press, Cisco Press, John Wiley & Sons, Syngress, Morgan Kaufmann, IBM Redbooks, Packt, Adobe Press, FT Press, Apress, Manning, New Riders, McGraw-Hill, Jones & Bartlett, Course Technology, and hundreds more. For more information about Safari Books Online, please visit us online.

How to Contact Us

Please address comments and questions concerning this book to the publisher:

O'Reilly Media, Inc.
1005 Gravenstein Highway North
Sebastopol, CA 95472
800-998-9938 (in the United States or Canada)
707-829-0515 (international or local)
707-829-0104 (fax)

We have a web page for this book, where we list errata, examples, and any additional information. You can access this page at *http://bit.ly/salt_essentials*.

To comment or ask technical questions about this book, send email to *bookquestions@oreilly.com*.

For more information about our books, courses, conferences, and news, see our website at *http://www.oreilly.com*.

Find us on Facebook: *http://facebook.com/oreilly*

Follow us on Twitter: *http://twitter.com/oreillymedia*

Watch us on YouTube: *http://www.youtube.com/oreillymedia*

Acknowledgments

This book would not have been possible without the support and encouragement of our friends and family. There are plenty of people who gave small hints and suggestions, but the book would not have been what it is without the help of David Boucha and Seth House from SaltStack. A big thank you goes to Ryan Lane and Seth House (again) for their review of the book; they found a number of pretty ugly mistakes. They also gave plenty of fantastic tips and some great advice on how many parts could be improved. We are indebted to them for their help.

CHAPTER 1

Introduction

What Is Salt?

Salt is a remote execution framework and configuration management system. It is similar to Chef, Puppet, Ansible, and cfengine. These systems are all written to solve the same basic problem: how do you maintain consistency across many machines, whether it is 2 machines or 20,000? What makes Salt different is that it accomplishes this high-level goal via a very fast and secure communication system. Its high-speed data bus allows Salt to manage just a few hosts or even a very large environment containing thousands of hosts. This is the very backbone of Salt. Once this encrypted communication channel is established, many more options open up. On top of this authenticated event bus is the remote execution engine. Then, continuing to build on existing layers, comes the state system. The state system uses the remote execution system, which, in turn, is layered on top of the secure event bus. This layering of functionality is what makes Salt so powerful.

But this is just the core of what Salt provides. Salt is written in Python, and its execution framework is just more Python. The default configuration uses a standard data format, YAML. Salt comes with a couple of other options if you don't want to use YAML. The power of Salt is in its extensibility. Most of Salt can easily be customized—everything from the format of the data files to the code that runs on each host to how data is exchanged. Salt provides powerful application programming interfaces (APIs) and easy ways to layer new code on top of existing modules. This code can either be run on the centralized coordination host (aka the *master*) or on the clients themselves (aka the *minions*). Salt will do the "heavy lifting" of determining which host should run which code based on a number of different *targeting* options.

High-Level Architecture

There are a few key terms that you need to understand before moving on. First, all of your hosts are called minions. Actions performed on them are usually coordinated via a centralized machine called the master. As a host, the master is also a minion to itself. In most cases, you will initiate commands on the master giving a *target*, the command to run, and any arguments. Salt will expand the target into a list of minions. In the simplest case, the target can be a single minion specified by its *minion ID*. You can also list several minion IDs, or use *globs* (*http://bit.ly/glob_programming*) to provide some pattern to match against. (For example, a simple * will match all minions.) You can even reach further into the minion's data and target based on the operating system, or the number of CPUs, or any custom metadata you set.

The basic design is a very simple client/server model. Salt runs as a daemon, or background, process. This is true for both the master and the minion. When the master process comes up, it provides a location (socket) where minions can "bind" and watch for commands. The minion is configured with the location—that is, the domain name system (DNS) or IP address—of the master. When the minion daemon starts, it connects to that master socket and listens for events. As previously mentioned, each minion has an ID. This ID must be unique so that the master can exchange data with only that minion, if desired. This ID is usually the hostname, but can be configured as something else. Once the minion connects to the master, there is an initial "handshake" process where the master needs to confirm that the minion matches the ID it is advertising.[1]

In the default case, this means you will need to manually confirm the minion. Once the minion ID is established, the master and minion can communicate along a ZeroMQ (*http://www.zeromq.org/*)[2] data bus. When the master sends out a command to ZeroMQ, it is said to "publish" events, and when the minions are listening to the data bus, they are said to "subscribe" to, or listen for, those events—hence the descriptor pub-sub.

When the master publishes a command, it simply puts it on the ZeroMQ bus for all of the minions to see. Each minion will then look at the command and the target (and the target type) to determine if it should run that command. If the minion determines that it does not match the combination of target and target type, then it will simply ignore that command. When the master sends a command out to the minions, it relies on the minions being able to identify the command via the target.

---

1 This handshake between the minions and the master is the same as the handshake used by SSH. But the handshake for Salt is simply implemented on top of ZeroMQ.

2 ZeroMQ is an open source, asynchronous messaging library aimed at large, distributed systems.

We have glossed over some details here. While the minions do listen on the data bus to match their ID and associated data (e.g., *grains*[3]) to the target (using the target type to determine which set of data to use), the master will verify that the target given does or does not match any minions. In the case of a match against the name (e.g., glob, regex, or simple list), the master will match the target with a list of IDs it has (via salt-key). But, for grain matching, the master will look at a local cache of the grains to determine if any minions match. This is similar for *pillar*[4] matching and for matching by IP address. All of that logic allows the master to build a list of minions that *should* respond to a given command. The master can then compare that list against the list of minions that return data and thus identify which minions did not respond in time. Also, the master can determine that no minions match the criteria given (target combined with target type) and thus not send any command.

This is only half of the communication. Once a minion has decided to execute the given command, it will return data to the master (see Figure 1-1). The first part of the communication, where the minions are listening for commands, is called *publish and subscribe*, or *pub-sub*. The minions all connect to a single port on the master to listen for these commands. But there is a second port on the master that all minions send back any data. This includes whether the command succeeded or not, and a variety of other data.

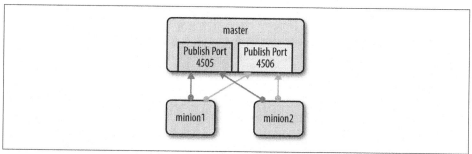

Figure 1-1. Communication between master and minions

This remote execution framework provides the basic toolset upon which other functionality is built. The most notable example is *salt states*. *States* are a way to manage configurations across all of your minions. A salt state defines how you want a given host to be configured. For example, you might want a list of packages installed on a

---

3 Grains are data about the minions, stored on the minions. They are discussed at length in Chapter 5.

4 Pillar is data about the minion stored on the master. This is also discussed at length in Chapter 5.

specific type of machine—for example, all web servers. Or maybe you want to have a number of users added on a shared development server. The state has those requirements enumerated, normally using YAML. Once you have the configuration defined, you give the state system the minions for which you want that particular configuration applied. The minions are defined through the same flexible targeting system mentioned earlier. A salt state gives you a very flexible way to define a "template" for setting up a given host.

Declarative Versus Imperative Configuration Management

There are two basic schools of thought on configuration management. In *imperative* management, you explicitly give Salt an ordered list of actions to perform. In *declarative* management, on the other hand, you merely give the desired *end state* and allow the system to figure out how best to enforce it.

The proponents of the declarative model argue that it simplifies the configuration and thus makes it easier to understand. Obviously, you will need to trust that the system is handling edge cases in the manner you expect. Also, if there are problems, you need to rely on the system to provide you with sufficient information to diagnose the root cause.

However, the imperative model is more natural to a programmer accustomed to providing a list of commands. The downside of it is that you must list all of the corner cases and how you want them handled.

A detailed discussion on this topic is beyond the scope of this book. However, Salt does provide the option to use either model. As you will see when we discuss how to extend Salt in Chapter 6, you can run commands explicitly using the remote execution environment (imperative) or you can specify your desired end state using the state system (declarative).

The last important architectural cornerstone of Salt is that all of the communication is done via a secure, encrypted channel. Earlier, we briefly mentioned that when a minion first connects to the master, there is a process whereby the minion is validated. The default process is that you must view the list and manually accept the known minions. Once the minion is validated, the minion and master exchange encryption keys. The encryption uses the industry-standard AES specification. The master will store the public key of every minion. It is therefore critical that you maintain tight security control on your master. Once the trust relationship is established, any communication between the master and all minions is secure. However, this security is dependent on that initial setup of trust and on the sustained security of the master. The minions, on the other hand, do not have any *global* secrets. If a minion is compromised, it will be able to watch the ZeroMQ data bus and see commands sent out to the minions. But that is all it will be able to do. The net result is that all data sent between the master and its minions remains secure. But while the communication channel is kept secure, you still need to maintain a tight security profile on your master.

Some Quick Examples

Let's run through a couple of quick examples so you can see what Salt can do.

System Management

A common use case for a remote execution framework is to install packages. With Salt, a single command can be used to install (or upgrade) packages across your entire infrastructure. With its powerful targeting syntax, you can install a package on all hosts, or only on CentOS 5.2 hosts, or maybe only on hosts with 24 CPUs.

Here is a simple example:

```
salt '*' pkg.install apache
```

This installs the Apache package on every host (*). If you want to target a list of minions based on information about the host (e.g., the operating system or some hardware attribute), you do so by using some data that the master keeps about each minion. This data coming from the minion (e.g., operating system) is called grains. But there is another type of data: *pillar* data. While grains are advertised by the minion back to the master, pillar data is stored on the master and is made available to each minion individually; that is, a minion cannot see any pillar data but its own. It is common for people new to Salt to ask about grains versus pillar data, so we will discuss them further in Chapter 5. For the moment, you can think of grains as metadata about the host (e.g., number of CPUs), while pillar is data the host needs (e.g., a database password). In other words, a minion *tells* the master what its grains are, while the minion *asks* the master for its pillar data. For now, just know that you can use either to define the target for a command.

Configuration Management

The central master can distribute files that describe how a system should be configured. As we've discussed, these descriptions are called *states*, and they are stored in simple YAML files called *SLS* (salt states). A state to manage the main index file for Apache might look like the following:

```
webserver_main_index_file:
  file.managed:
    - name: /var/www/index.html
    - source: salt://webserver/main.html
```

The first line is simply a unique identifier. Next comes the command to enforce. The description (i.e., state) says that a file is managed by Salt. The source of the file is on the Salt master in the location given. (Salt comes with a very lightweight *file server* that can manage files it needs—for example, configuration files, Java WAR files, or Windows installers.) The next two lines describe where the file should end up on the minion (*/var/www/index.html*), and where on the master to find the file (*.../webserver/main.html*). (The path for the source of the file is relative to the *file root* for the master. That will be explained later, but just know that the source is not an absolute file path, while the destination is an absolute path.)

The *file server* is a mechanism for Salt to send files out to the minions. Larger files will be broken up into chunks to be more easily sent over the encrypted communication channel. This makes the file server very handy. But keep in mind that Salt's file server is not meant to be a generic file server like NFS or CIFS.

Salt comes with a number of built-in *state modules* to help create the descriptions that define how an entire host should be configured. The `file` state module is just a simple introduction. You can also define the users that should be present, the services (applications) that should be running, and which packages should be installed. Not only is there a wealth of state modules built in to Salt, but you can also write your own, which we'll cover in Chapter 6.

You may have noticed that when we installed the package using the execution module directly, we gave a target host: every host (*). But when we showed the state, there was no target minion given. In the state system, there is high-level abstraction that specifies which host should have which states. This is called the *top file*. While the states give a *recipe* for how a host should look, the top file says which hosts should have which recipes. We will discuss this in much more detail in Chapter 4.

A Brief History

Like many projects and ideas, Salt was born out of necessity. I (Tom) had created a couple of in-house remote execution incarnations over the years. But I found that these and the other open sourced options didn't quite have the power I was looking for. I then decided to base a new system on the fast ZeroMQ messaging layer. As I began adding more and more functionality, the state system just naturally appeared. Then, as the community grew, more and more functionality was added. But the core remote execution framework remained extensible.

> ### Why the Name "Salt"?
>
> There is a lot of speculation over why we chose the name Salt. SaltStack is based out of Salt Lake City, so that is a popular theory. But the name of the framework is not related to the city of its birth. When looking for a name for the project, I was watching the *Lord of the Rings* and the topic of "salted pork" came up. Then it hit me: salt makes everything better. Thus the name Salt—because it makes system management better.

Topology Options

Thus far, we have discussed Salt only as a single master with a number of connected minions. However, this is not the only option. You can divide up your minions and have them talk to an intermediate host called a *syndication master*. An example use case is when you have clusters of hosts that are geographically dispersed. You may have high-latency links between the clusters, but each cluster has a fast network locally. For example, you have a bunch of hosts in New York, another large cluster in Sydney, maybe another grouping in London, and, finally, all of your development in San Francisco. A syndication master will act as a proxy for the master.

You may even decide that you only want to use Salt's execution modules and states without any master at all. A *masterless minion* setup is briefly discussed in "Masterless Minions" on page 135.

Lastly, you may want to allow some users to harness the power Salt provides without giving them access directly to the main master. The *peer publisher* system allows you to give special access to some minions. This could allow you to let developers run deployment commands without giving them access to the entire set of tools that Salt provides.

 The various topologies mentioned here are not necessarily mutually exclusive. You can use them individually, or even mix and match them. For example, you could have the majority of your infrastructure managed using the standard *master–minion* topology, but then have your more security-sensitive host managed via a *masterless* setup. Salt's basic usage and core functionality remain the same; only the implementation details differ.

Extending Salt

Out of the box, Salt is extremely powerful and comes with a number of modules to help you administer a variety of operating systems. However, no matter how powerful the system is or how complete it attempts to be, it cannot be all things to all people. As a result, Salt's extensibility underpins the entire system. You can dynamically generate the data in the configuration files using a templating engine (e.g., Jinja or Mako), a DSL, or just straight code. Or you can write your own custom execution modules using Python. Salt provides a number of libraries and data structures, which allow custom modules to peer into the core of the Salt system to extract data or even run other modules. Once you have the concept of extending using modules, you can then write your own states to enforce whatever logic you see fit.

As powerful as custom modules or custom states may be, they are only the beginning of what you can change. As previously mentioned, the format of the state files is YAML. But you can add your own *renderer* to convert any data file into a data structure that Salt can handle. Even the data about a host (i.e., grains and pillar) can be altered and customized.

All of these customizations do not live in their own sandbox. They are available to the rest of Salt, and the rest of Salt is available to them. Thus, you can write your own custom execution module and call it using the state system. Or you can write your own state that uses only the modules that ship with Salt.

All of this makes Salt very powerful and a bit overwhelming. This book is here to guide you through the basics and give some very simple examples of what Salt can do. Just to sweeten the pot, Salt has a very active community that is here to help you when you run into obstacles.

Are you ready to get salted?

CHAPTER 2

Quick Start: First Taste of Salt

There are a lot of terms and commands that are specific to Salt. Rather than discuss them at an abstract level, let's dive right in and run some very simple commands. In order to proceed, you will need several minions set up and configured to communicate with your Salt master. In this book's companion code, there is a *Vagrant* file you can use to quickly set up five hosts: a single master and four minions. Most details are given in Appendix A. If you already have your hosts set up and Salt installed, you can skip ahead to "Starting Up" on page 11.

 If you used the companion code's Vagrant configuration, the Salt daemons are already started. However, you should still read "Starting Up" on page 11 to become familiar with the process.

Single-Master Setup

The most straightforward and common use of Salt is to have a few minions attached to a single master. We will set up a single master and then configure a couple of minions to talk to that master.

But first we need to figure out how to install Salt. Both minion and master share a great deal of code. We will install all of the core libraries on all hosts: minions and our single master. There are some command-line utilities that make sense only to run on the master (e.g., `salt-run` and `salt`). If they are installed on a host without the correct master configuration, they will report an error and do nothing. It is not harmful to have the master-specific utilities installed on the minions, but it can lead to confusion. Thus, we will have slightly different installs for the master and the minions to help prevent any confusion. But all hosts will have the core libraries installed. Then the master will have some additional code (mostly the command-line interface, or CLIs) installed.

The examples in this book use both Ubuntu and CentOS minions. As a result, we are concerned only with the *RPM* and *apt* packages. However, Salt supports a wide variety of platforms, and this list is ever-changing. Therefore, we recommend that you check the Salt documentation (*http://bit.ly/salt_install*) for how to install on your specific platform.

Again, Appendix A has some instructions for how to start up a master and four additional minions using Vagrant. These instructions use the book's utilities located on GitHub (*https://github.com/craig5/salt-essentials-utils*).

From Packages

It is assumed that you have some basic familiarity with the package system on your particular operating system. But, to just give you a quick flavor of what is involved, here are the basic instructions for installing using *yum* (and *RPM*).

First, you need to verify that the packages are available via the repositories you have configured:

```
[vagrant@master ~]$ sudo yum list salt salt-master salt-minion
Available Packages
salt.noarch                    2014.7.0-3.el6              epel
salt-master.noarch             2014.7.0-3.el6              epel
salt-minion.noarch             2014.7.0-3.el6              epel
```

You need to install the base Salt package and the minion on every host:

```
# yum install -y salt salt-minion
```

Also, on the host you designate as the master, you will need the *salt-master* package as well:

```
# yum install -y salt-master
```

Note that the packages are not in the main CentOS repositories. But they are available via EPEL (Extra Packages for Enterprise Linux). You can install the EPEL repositories very easily with:

```
sudo rpm -Uvh \
    http://download.fedoraproject.org/pub/epel/6/i386/epel-release-6-8.noarch.rpm
```

Again, this is merely a quick example of how to install on an RPM-based operating system. The installation instructions on Salt's documentation pages will provide details for other supported operating systems.

Bootstrap Script

Since the installation is so varied across so many different platforms, a simplified installation script was created. It lives at a simple URL: *http://bootstrap.saltstack.com*. This URL will provide a *bash* script that supports the installation of Salt on a couple of dozen different UNIX-like variants. You can find the current list of supported operating systems on the Salt bootstrap page (*http://bit.ly/salt_bootstrap*).

This bootstrap script is meant to make it easy to install Salt, but it is not the most secure method for installation. Therefore, it is not recommended for production environments. It is simply an easy way for you to get Salt installed so you can start learning. Once you are familiar with Salt, you should be able to install it using the package manager of your choosing or even directly from the source on GitHub if you desire.

Starting Up

There are two main daemons:

- */usr/bin/salt-minion*
- */usr/bin/salt-master*

Before we start up the minions, we need to make sure they can communicate with the master. The default setting is to use a host named simply *salt*. The basic minion configuration is located in */etc/salt/minion*. Like so much of Salt, it is a YAML-formatted file. You need to configure each minion with the DNS name or IP address of your Salt master:

```
[vagrant@master ~]$ sudo grep '#master:' /etc/salt/minion
#master: salt
```

You will find that most of the defaults in both the minion and master configuration files are included as comments.

If you have the flexibility to change your DNS to use a master named *salt*, then you can leave the configuration as is. Otherwise, you will need to uncomment that line and replace the value with either the DNS name or IP address of your Salt master.

Next we need to start the `salt-master` daemon process on the master host:

```
[vagrant@master ~]$ sudo service salt-master start
Starting salt-master daemon:                           [  OK  ]
```

Then we need to start up the `salt-minion` daemon process on all hosts (including the master):

```
[vagrant@master ~]$ sudo service salt-minion start
Starting salt-minion daemon:                           [  OK  ]
```

How the minion ID is computed

The Salt minions will create their own ID based on their hostname. However, *hostname* doesn't always mean the same thing to everyone. For example, is it the fully qualified domain name (FQDN) or not?

When the minion starts up, if the ID has not already been set, the minion will try to set it to a value that is not *localhost* using the following order:

1. The Python function `socket.getfqdn()`.
2. Check */etc/hostname*.
3. Check */etc/hosts*.

If none of those yields a name that is not *localhost*, then Salt will inspect the IP addresses configured on the host. It will take the first publicly routable address. It is critical that every minion has a unique ID. Also, the minion will cache that ID in */etc/salt/minion_id*. If you change the hostname, be aware that the cache file will not automatically update. If you change the hostname, stop the `salt-minion` daemon, delete that file, and then restart the `salt-minion` process. That should regenerate the cache file using the new hostname.

Be careful about firewalls. The minions need to talk to the master on ports 4505 and 4506. In the previous chapter, we talked about pub-sub and the return data. Those two ports are the communication channels Salt uses. The first is called the *publish port* (`publish_port`), and the second is called the *return port* (`ret_port`).

If everything is working properly, you should see a message like the following in the *minion's* logs:

```
[vagrant@master ~]$ sudo tail -1 /var/log/salt/minion
2015-01-20 00:08:15,750 [salt.crypt ][ERROR    ] The Salt Master has
cached the public key for this node, this Salt minion will wait for
10 seconds before attempting to re-authenticate
```

The minion actually runs the commands on each host. The master helps coordinate which hosts run which commands and then deals with the returned data. As a result, the master does have a minion process running on it. Since the majority of the work we are going to do will be done on the master, we will also use the master host to show some properties about minions.

At this point, the minions are just waiting for the master to confirm that they are authorized. Next we will introduce the basic Salt command-line utilities.

Basic Commands

Interacting with Salt means using one of the command-line tools. There are several commands, but for the moment we care only about the following four:

- */usr/bin/salt*
- */usr/bin/salt-key*
- */usr/bin/salt-run*
- */usr/bin/salt-call*

The one you will care the most about is the basic `salt` command.

salt: The Main Workhorse

A simple yet powerful way to automate is to run a single command on many hosts. This is exactly where the `salt` command comes in. The `salt` command runs on the master and takes as arguments the minions you want to affect—that is, the target and whatever command you want to run on those minions.

There are many ways to tell the Salt system which minions you want to affect, ranging from a simple list of minion IDs to using data from the minions, aka grains. For example, you can target all hosts running RHEL 6.4. For now, we are going to run our commands on all minions. For this we just need a simple glob: `*`. We'll discuss the different options for selecting minions later in "Minion Targeting" on page 24.

The format of the Salt command is `salt` *target command*. For example:

```
[vagrant@master ~]$ sudo salt minion1.example test.ping
```

This simple example says to run `test.ping` on the minion named `minion1.example`. The argument `test.ping` is an *execution module*. This is one of the basic elements of Salt: remote execution. (Execution modules are explained in more detail in the next chapter.) In this specific case, all `test.ping` does is execute the simplest of commands: return `True`. If the minion is functioning normally, that code will execute on the minion(s), and the return value, `True`, will be received by the master. This is normally the easiest way (and the one with the least overhead) to verify that a given set of minions is working.

The core Salt code comes with a wealth of execution modules, including ones for package management, crontab modification, iptable editing, and user management. This is only a small sample of the commands available in the core package. You can find the complete list of modules (*http://bit.ly/salt_modules*) on the Salt web page.

Even more power comes from writing your own execution modules. They are just Python code, but they also have access to some Salt-specific data structures, which makes the combination extremely powerful. In Chapter 6 we discuss how to write your own custom modules.

salt-key: Key Management

We have been discussing the encrypted channel over which the master and minions communicate. We have also mentioned that there needs to be an initial *trust relationship* established. The master keeps a record of all minions and the state of that trust. Each minion will be in one of three states: accepted, unaccepted, or rejected. When a minion first connects, it is put into the unaccepted state. At that point the key can either be accepted or rejected. We can manage the various states using the salt-key command. Let's take a look at how our example minions look after the salt-minion process has started:

```
[vagrant@master ~]$ sudo salt-key
Accepted Keys:
Unaccepted Keys:
master.example
minion1.example
minion2.example
minion3.example
minion4.example
Rejected Keys:
```

As you can see, all of the minions are sitting in the unaccepted state. Without any arguments, salt-key will simply list all of the states and then each minion in each of those states. You can view just the keys in the unaccepted state using the --list argument:

```
[vagrant@master ~]$ sudo salt-key --list=unaccepted
Unaccepted Keys:
master.example
minion1.example
minion2.example
minion3.example
minion4.example
```

You can accept a key by simply adding the --accept flag with the ID of the minion you want to accept:

```
[vagrant@master ~]$ sudo salt-key --accept=master.example --yes
The following keys are going to be accepted:
Unaccepted Keys:
master.example
Key for minion master.example accepted.
```

In this case, we are simply going to accept all of the keys. Rather than accepting each minion individually, we can accept all of the minions in the unaccepted state using the --accept-all argument:

```
[vagrant@master ~]$ sudo salt-key --accept-all
The following keys are going to be accepted:
Unaccepted Keys:
minion1.example
minion2.example
minion3.example
minion4.example
Proceed? [n/Y] y
Key for minion minion1.example accepted.
Key for minion minion2.example accepted.
Key for minion minion3.example accepted.
Key for minion minion4.example accepted.
```

Now, if you run salt-key again, you will see all of the keys have moved into the accepted state:

```
[vagrant@master ~]$ sudo salt-key
Accepted Keys:
master.example
minion1.example
minion2.example
minion3.example
minion4.example
Unaccepted Keys:
Rejected Keys:
```

There are options to remove keys, generate fingerprints, and more. (A fingerprint is a standard method in public-key cryptography to give an ID to a public key. This fingerprint is usually a simple hash of the public key and makes referencing the key easier simply because of the shorter string.) There is even an option to pre-generate a key pair based on a minion ID. This would be very handy if you know you are about to add several minions and want to prepare ahead of time. However, if you pre-generate the minion's key pair, you will still need to have that key pair installed on the minion. There are a number of strategies for managing a large number of minions, but they are beyond the scope of this book. Here we will just use the manual process of managing minion keys.

If you want to add another layer of security, you can add the `master_finger` option to your minion's configuration. This allows you to set the fingerprint of the master's encryption key in the minion. You can find the fingerprint of the master's key by running the following command on the Salt master:

```
salt-key -f master.pub
```

Refer to the example minion configuration file (*http://bit.ly/ minion_config*) that comes with Salt for more information.

salt-call: Execution on the Minion

In our discussion so far, we have talked about centralized management. But remember that the main purpose of the master is the centralized management and control of the minions. The remote execution modules actually run *on* the minions themselves. You can take advantage of this and run commands directly using the `salt-call` command. `salt-call` will run an execution module or enforce a state, but only on *localhost*. All of Salt's code is available along with the custom data via grains and pillar. Let's look at a simple example:

```
[vagrant@minion1 ~]$ sudo salt-call test.ping
local:
    True
```

One of the first things you'll notice is that, unlike with the `salt` command, there is no set of minions supplied with `salt-call`. That is because `salt-call` will only work on *localhost*, so a target has no meaning when you use `salt-call`.

Since we also have a minion running on the Salt master, you can definitely run `salt-call` on the master, but it affects only that master system itself; nothing changes on any other minions.

One of the big advantages of using `salt-call` is that your commands are isolated to just a single host. This really helps with debugging. You can pass the `--log-level` flag and set it to `debug` to get more information about what is happening:

```
[vagrant@minion1 ~]$ sudo salt-call --log-level=debug disk.percent /
[DEBUG   ] Reading configuration from /etc/salt/minion
<snip>
[INFO    ] Executing command 'df -P' in directory '/root'
[DEBUG   ] output: Filesystem  1024-blocks    Used Available Capacity Mounted on
/dev/mapper/VolGroup-lv_root 39710104 875364   36810908  3% /
tmpfs                         251080       0     251080  0% /dev/shm
/dev/sda1                     487652   25039     437013  6% /boot
<snip>
local:
    3%
```

When we introduced the topic of pub-sub, we mentioned that it was only half of the communication—namely, it was how a command got to the minions. There is also a channel used for sending data back to the master. There are two different sockets on the master, on two different ports (specifically, 4505 for the publish port and 4506 for the return port). While the `salt-call` command runs locally, it will still attempt to *return* data to the master via the return port. If you truly want to *only* run locally, you just have to add the `--local` flag. This will ignore returning data to the master:

```
[vagrant@minion1 ~]$ sudo salt-call --local test.ping
local:
    True
```

Not only does `salt-call` come in handy for debugging, but there is also a standard layout where only `salt-call` is used. This is called masterless minions and is discussed in Chapter 9.

salt-run: Coordination of Jobs on the Master

What happens if you need to coordinate a number of tasks across many minions? For example, say you want to deploy a new application to 10 hosts, but you only want to take one down at a time. When you use the `salt` command with a target set of minions, the command is sent asynchronously to every minion. But if you want to run a command sequentially across many minions, a *runner* can help.[1] The `salt-run` command is a *master-only* command. It does not take a target set of minions. It is used for coordinating commands across a predetermined set of hosts or to access data that is available only on the master itself. An example is the `manage` runner:

```
[vagrant@master ~]$ sudo salt-run manage.up
master.example
minion1.example
minion2.example
minion3.example
minion4.example
```

Again, no minions are specified on the command line. This particular module, `manage.up`, uses the `test.ping` execution module, which we have already seen, to determine whether a minion is healthy. Internally, it executes something similar to `salt * test.ping`. It then reports all of the minions that return `True`.

---

1 Runners are discussed in detail in Chapter 7.

Terminology: Modules and Functions

Up until now, we have been a little loose with some of our terms—notably, *execution modules*. An execution module is actually a collection of execution functions. You run specific execution functions on a minion. For example, the `test` execution module has a function called `ping`. So, you run the `test.ping` execution function on a minion. Specifically, an execution module is a Python file. Each public method defined in that Python file is exposed as an execution function. Again, in our example, when you call `test.ping`, Salt looks for a file called *test.py* and then for a public function called `ping` inside that file. These terms are not hard and fast; there is some fudging. You may see references to "running the `foo.bar` module." While that's not as specific as saying, "running the `bar` execution function from the `foo` execution module," hopefully you can see how that shorthand can be easier, albeit more ambiguous.

Summary of Commands

To recap, there are four basic commands:

- `salt`
- `salt-key`
- `salt-run`
- `salt-call`

The first three are all directly executed on the master. Then, `salt-call` is run on the minion itself. (Remember, the master is also a minion.)

The first, `salt`, is the command you will use most of the time. It will take a minion target, the execution function you want to call, and then any optional arguments for that particular function. One important note: when you run commands using `salt`, it merely coordinates the sending of the job to each minion. The `salt-master` daemon will then collect any data returned from the minions.[2]

The execution module *runs on the minion itself*, not on the master. This is important if you need additional third-party libraries installed or there are additional requirements (e.g., certain users are present).[3] The next command, `salt-key`, handles the

---

[2] Even though the `salt` command does not *itself* process the return data, it does wait for the data to be returned to the `salt-master` daemon. This is a small, but important, distinction.

[3] In the case of runner modules, since the code is executed on the *master*, any dependent libraries must be installed there.

management of the minion keys on the master. We will discuss key management in a little more depth in the following section.

If you need to coordinate among many minions, or you need the code to run on the master, you can use the `salt-run` command. It calls a class of modules called runners. The key difference is that it runs only on the master, while the `salt` command sends code to execute on each minion.

Lastly, there is an option to run a module directly on a specific minion. For this, you would use the `salt-call` CLI tool. While it will return data to the master by default, you can also run it in *local-only* mode. It really helps when you are debugging problems; you can focus on one minion at a time when trying to narrow down the root cause of a failure.

Key Management

All communication between the minions and the master is encrypted via AES encryption. The first step in establishing the encrypted channel is to exchange keys. When a minion first comes online and connects to the master, the minion will receive the master's public key and then send its public key to the master. This entire process is internal to the Salt master and Salt minions, and you only have to worry about which keys to accept and/or reject. It is important to understand the basics of this communication because it is essential to how Salt works.

 These keys are the minion IDs. These IDs must be unique. In order to avoid any conflicts, it is usually considered best practice to use the FQDN as the minion ID. However, this can be a little tedious if you have a very long domain name. In the end, Salt only cares that each minion ID is *unique*.

Viewing Keys

We briefly showed how to list all keys earlier. This is the default behavior of `salt-key`. So, barring any arguments, it will just list all the status of all keys and each minion in each state.

When looking for only keys in a specific category, you can provide an argument to the `--list` flag. For example, setting that flag to `acc` (accepted) will show only the accepted keys:

```
[vagrant@master ~]$ sudo salt-key --list=acc
Accepted Keys:
master.example
minion1.example
minion2.example
```

```
minion3.example
minion4.example
```

In addition to showing you the keys by name, the `salt-key` command can provide
the fingerprints of each key file:

```
[vagrant@master ~]$ sudo salt-key --finger master.example
Accepted Keys:
master.example:  ae:45:a3:00:81:b2:46:bd:a6:32:29:87:ac:a9:3b:86
```

There is also a `--finger-all` argument available, which will list the fingerprint of all
keys in all states. This includes the master's public and private keys.

When there are issues with the key exchange, the fingerprints help to identify which
minion key is which. (For example, say you happen to rename a hostname, but do not
remove the cached ID on the minion *and* restart the `salt-minion` daemon. In this
case, you can get both fingerprints: the one stored on the master and the one used by
the minion itself. Those two fingerprints should match.) To view the fingerprint of
the key on the minion itself, you can turn to `salt-call` and the `key.finger` module:

```
[vagrant@master ~]$ sudo salt-call --local key.finger
local:
    ae:45:a3:00:81:b2:46:bd:a6:32:29:87:ac:a9:3b:86
```

You can also verify the fingerprint of the master on any problem minions:

```
[vagrant@master ~]$ sudo salt-call --local key.finger_master
local:
    d3:60:cc:56:12:c2:90:a1:ee:a0:ae:a9:cb:9d:3d:ea
```

Once you have the fingerprints for the keys on each minion (using `salt-call`) and
the fingerprints stored on the master (using `salt-key --finger-all`), you can compare them to make sure everything is in agreement.

Accepting Keys

Before the key exchange takes place, the minion keys (on the master) are put into an
unaccepted state. You learned about this in the earlier discussion of the `salt-key`
command. We can go back to this state by simply deleting all of the keys:

```
[vagrant@master ~]$ sudo salt-key --delete-all
The following keys are going to be deleted:
Accepted Keys:
master.example
minion1.example
minion2.example
minion3.example
minion4.example
Proceed? [N/y] y
Key for minion master.example deleted.
Key for minion minion1.example deleted.
```

```
Key for minion minion2.example deleted.
Key for minion minion3.example deleted.
Key for minion minion4.example deleted.
```

At this point, all of the minion keys have been deleted and the minions need to be restarted on each host, so they must authenticate again with the master:

```
[vagrant@master ~]$ sudo service salt-minion restart
Stopping salt-minion daemon:                           [  OK  ]
Starting salt-minion daemon:                           [  OK  ]
```

(You'll need to restart the salt-minion daemon on each host.)

```
[vagrant@master ~]$ sudo salt-key
Accepted Keys:
Unaccepted Keys:
master.example
minion1.example
minion2.example
minion3.example
minion4.example
Rejected Keys:
```

As you can see, all minions are back in the unaccepted state. Earlier, we showed an example of accepting only the master key and then all unaccepted minions. The --accept flag also accepts globbing if you want to match a group of minions all at once:

```
[vagrant@master ~]$ sudo salt-key --accept=master\*
The following keys are going to be accepted:
Unaccepted Keys:
master.example
Proceed? [n/Y] y
Key for minion master.example accepted.
```

Rejecting Keys

You can also reject keys for minions:

```
[vagrant@master ~]$ sudo salt-key --reject='minion1*'
The following keys are going to be rejected:
Unaccepted Keys:
minion1.example
Proceed? [n/Y] y
Key for minion minion1.example rejected.
```

Now, listing all of the keys is a little more interesting:

```
[vagrant@master ~]$ sudo salt-key
Accepted Keys:
master.example
Unaccepted Keys:
minion2.example
minion3.example
minion4.example
```

```
Rejected Keys:
minion1.example
```

Notice we used a slightly different syntax when using the wildcard pattern in the previous examples. This is specific to the shell and is not a product of Salt itself. In order to pass the asterisk (*) into Salt, you need to escape it from the shell. Either surrounding it with single quotes or preceding it with a backslash (\) will work. We use both throughout the book. You can use whichever is most comfortable to you.

By default, `salt-key` acts only on keys that are in the unaccepted state. Let's first try to accept *all* of the keys and see what happens:

```
[vagrant@master ~]$ sudo salt-key --accept-all
The following keys are going to be accepted:
Unaccepted Keys:
minion2.example
minion3.example
minion4.example
Proceed? [n/Y] y
Key for minion minion2.example accepted.
Key for minion minion3.example accepted.
Key for minion minion4.example accepted.

[vagrant@master ~]$ sudo salt-key
Accepted Keys:
master.example
minion2.example
minion3.example
minion4.example
Unaccepted Keys:
Rejected Keys:
minion1.example
```

Notice that even though you added the `--accept-all` flag, `salt-key` accepted only the keys that were in the unaccepted state. If you really want to accept *all* keys, not just those keys waiting for a decision (i.e., those in the unaccepted state), you need to add the `--include-all` flag:

```
[vagrant@master ~]$ sudo salt-key --include-all --accept-all
The following keys are going to be accepted:
Rejected Keys:
minion1.example
Proceed? [n/Y] y
Key for minion minion1.example accepted.
```

That same logic holds for *rejecting* keys. When you accept or reject keys, it is assumed that you are trying to decide what to do about keys that are *pending* a decision (aka unaccepted), not keys that have already been accepted or rejected.

Now we have gotten our minions back into the accepted state, so we can discuss some additional details about the keys themselves.

Key Files

The keys are stored in a *pki* directory. The default locations are */etc/salt/pki/master* and */etc/salt/pki/minion*.

PKI stands for *public key infrastructure*. It is a very common term in the industry, and you will see it used in many contexts other than Salt.

The minion stores its public and private keys as well as the public key of the master. Likewise, the master stores its public and private keys as well as the public key of every minion. To be clear, the minion and master keys are different. So, in the case of the master, we are talking about four total keys: the master's public and private keys, and the public and private keys for the minion running on the master itself.

On the minion, the layout is pretty straightforward, as shown in Table 2-1.

Table 2-1. Minion files and descriptions

Minion files	Summary
/etc/salt/pki/minion/minion.{pub,pem}	Minion's public and private keys
/etc/salt/pki/minion/minion_master.pub	The public key of the master stored on the minion

However, the master needs to categorize the minion keys based on whether they have been accepted or not. The filepaths give away their use, as you can see in Table 2-2.

Table 2-2. Master files and descriptions

Master files	Summary
/etc/salt/pki/master/master.{pub,pem}	Master's public and private keys
/etc/salt/pki/master/minions	Public keys of every accepted minion
/etc/salt/pki/master/minions_pre	Public keys of every unaccepted minion
/etc/salt/pki/master/minions_rejected	Public keys of every rejected minion

The minion public keys that the master records are stored in files by their minion ID. As the state is manipulated via salt-key (e.g., new keys are accepted), these files are then moved from one directory to another.[4] While it is handy to know some of those details, in practice, it is rare that you will ever have to touch these files directly.

Minion Targeting

We have referred to the *targeting* of minions multiple times. The target is used in the main salt command as the first argument. (We briefly mentioned that targeting is also used in *states*. We will discuss states in detail in Chapter 4. Just be aware that targeting is used for more than just the salt command.) Now, we will look at the options for how you can target using different attributes.

In our testing setup, we have a master and four additional minions. The following examples assume the setup shown in Table 2-3.

Table 2-3. Testing setup for minion targeting

ID	Master?	Operating system
master.example	Yes	CentOS 6.6
minion1.example	No	CentOS 6.6
minion2.example	No	CentOS 6.6
minion3.example	No	Ubuntu 14.04
minion4.example	No	Ubuntu 14.04

You can use any mix of minions that you need. You will just need to adjust the outputs of the examples accordingly. Also, we will be using the test.ping module heavily; this is a simple execution module that we have already introduced. There are multiple ways of targeting your minions. We are going to discuss the most common. This is not an exhaustive list, but rather merely some examples to get you familiar with how you can target commands to different collections of minions.

Minion ID

The simplest way to target is to specify minions based on ID:

---

[4] These files can be managed directly without the use of salt-key. They are just files in the locations mentioned here, but the details are beyond the scope of this book.

```
[vagrant@master ~]$ sudo salt minion1.example test.ping
minion1.example:
    True
```

List (-L)

Next, you can provide a comma-separated list of minion IDs:

```
[vagrant@master ~]$ sudo salt -L master.example,minion1.example test.ping
master.example:
    True
minion1.example:
    True
```

Glob

Simple, shell-style globs can be expanded to a list of minions. As we discussed earlier, an asterisk will expand to every known minion:

```
[vagrant@master ~]$ sudo salt '*' test.ping
minion1.example:
    True
minion3.example:
    True
minion4.example:
    True
minion2.example:
    True
master.example:
    True
```

 As you can clearly see in this example, the minions are not expected to return in any given order. The order is simply the first minion to send data back on the *return* socket.

You can also combine a glob with the minion ID:

```
[vagrant@master ~]$ sudo salt 'min*' test.ping
minion4.example:
    True
minion1.example:
    True
minion2.example:
    True
minion3.example:
    True
```

Regular Expression (-E)

Regular expressions allow for more complex patterns:

```
[vagrant@master ~]$ sudo salt -E 'minion(1|2)\.example' test.ping
minion1.example:
    True
minion2.example:
    True
```

This is a pretty simple regular expression. It just says:

1. Match anything starting with minion,

2. Then match either a 1 or a 2,

3. And then match anything ending with *.example.*

If you have a strong naming scheme, you can do powerful matching using regular expressions.

Grains (-G)

The minions will gather information about the operating system (and the environment in general) and present it to the user as grains. *Grains* are a simple data structure that allows you to target based on some underlying aspect of the systems you are running. (Grains will be discussed in detail in Chapter 5.) For example, grains provide the operating system name (e.g., CentOS) and the version (e.g., 6.6). This allows you to send a command to, say, upgrade the *Apache* package only on CentOS 6.6 hosts.

 It is important to note that the grains are loaded when the Salt minion starts. Grains are meant for static data. There are ways to load grains more dynamically, discussed in Chapter 5.

Let's see a quick example using the operating system name. We can ping only the CentOS hosts:

```
[vagrant@master ~]$ sudo salt -G 'os:CentOS' test.ping
master.example:
    True
minion2.example:
    True
minion1.example:
    True
```

And then likewise with the Ubuntu minions:

```
[vagrant@master ~]$ sudo salt -G 'os:Ubuntu' test.ping
minion4.example:
    True
minion3.example:
    True
```

Compound (-C)

The preceding methods of targeting minions are very powerful. But what if you want to combine several types in one command? That is where the *compound matcher* comes in. You can combine any of the other matchers in one command. The compound matcher works using simple prefixes for each type. Let's look at a simple example:

```
[vagrant@master ~]$ sudo salt -C 'master* or G@os:Ubuntu' test.ping
minion4.example:
    True
minion3.example:
    True
master.example:
    True
```

The different types of matchers are identified with a single capital letter followed by the at sign (@). In our example we used a grains matcher, G@, followed by the name and value of the grain, os:Ubuntu, just as in the grains example in the previous section.[5] We also used a standard globbing type: master*. Notice there was no single letter prefix, however. Just as with the salt command, a minion ID and/or a glob is the default matcher if nothing else is specified. Lastly, we need to combine the two types of matches using the or operator. (You can use the standard Boolean operators: and, or, and not.) Combining the other matchers is extremely powerful, and we have only scratched the surface of what is available.

Targeting Summary

We have shown some of the major ways you can target your minions. However, there are a few others. For example, you can target by IP address or via node groups. Node groups are an arbitrary list of minions defined in the master's configuration file. The previous examples will take you far. But be aware that there are other options for *targeting* your minions, and this is a list that can grow over time.

---

[5] The complete list of single-letter IDs used in compound matchers can be found at *http://bit.ly/compound_matchers*.

Additional Remote Execution Details

We have discussed pub-sub a few times. But, as it is so critical to how Salt works, let's give a quick review. The master will *publish* events onto a messaging bus and the minions are *subscribed*, listening for those events. The minion will then look at the target of the event to decide if it needs to do anything else. At the core of Salt is the messaging bus, ZeroMQ. The master sets up two sockets. The first is called the `publish_port` (default value: 4505). This is where the master publishes commands. The minions subscribe to that port, looking for commands to execute. It's important to note that once the command is sent to the minions, there is no further communication on that channel; that is, the communication channel is totally asynchronous. These command packets are kept very small to minimize the amount of network overhead.

These packets are serialized through *msgpack*, a very small and efficient binary serialization format. It is similar to JSON in the element types it supports. However, it will compress the data structure into the smallest packet possible. As a result, it will impose some restrictions on the sizes of some of its types. You don't really need to know much more than the fact that it exists. Every packet sent to and from the master and the minions will be encoded into the *msgpack* format.

> For more information, you can reference the *msgpack* website (*http://msgpack.org/*).

The minions will inspect the packets and determine whether a packet is destined for them. The minions are "smart" in that they decide which packets to act on, not the master. Once the minions have analyzed the packet and performed any actions, they will need to report any results back to the master. The minion will return data to the master on a different socket called the `ret_port` (default value: 4506). How this data is processed by the master is controlled via a *returner*. We will briefly discuss how this can be changed, but there are some pros and cons to changing the returner. (A thorough discussion is beyond the scope of this book.)

Conclusion

We have given a high-level overview of what Salt can do and its basic commands. Now, we need to expand on these fundamental concepts to show how you can leverage Salt in your infrastructure. The core functionality that ships with Salt is very powerful. But the real power comes into play when you start customizing Salt.

CHAPTER 3

Execution Modules: The Functional Foundation

Salt comes with a rich set of execution modules and execution functions that allow you to administer many common tasks on your systems. All of these routines are simply Python. There isn't any custom language; it's just Python. The Salt libraries are exposed to these modules and functions, giving them access to the innards of the Salt system. Alongside the standard, built-in modules is the ability to add functionality with your own code.

The list of modules built in to Salt is extensive. The best place to look is on the main documentation site (*http://docs.saltstack.com/*).[1] We have already been using the `test.ping` module pretty heavily in our examples up until now. It would take an entire book to describe all of the modules in detail, so we are going to cherry-pick a few of the most heavily used ones to give you a taste of what is available. But we sincerely encourage you to examine the list on the Salt web pages. The list grows almost every day, with both new modules and new functionality added to existing modules.

sys: Information and Documentation About Modules

Whether you are an experienced user or brand new to Salt, you are eventually going to need to see some documentation. The `sys` module offers a lot of insight into the modules and functions loaded. We have mentioned several times already that the modules are actually executed on the minions themselves. The minions may be in different states. They may have different dependent libraries loaded or a different

---

1 At the top of the web page, you should see a link for "all Salt modules." That will take you to the complete list of execution modules available for the current version of Salt.

configuration. Also, the Salt modules loaded may simply be out of date. (Later in this chapter we will introduce the `saltutil` module, which contains functions for making sure your minions are up to date.) The `sys` modules will give you additional insight into the modules and functions on a given minion.

sys.doc Basic Documentation

It is considered a best practice to document all the publicly visible functions within a module. The `sys.doc` function will expose the docstrings in each function. As with all functions, we can use either the `salt` CLI on the master (with a list of minions) or the `salt-call` CLI directly on each minion itself.

 Python's docstrings are very similar in concept to Javadoc. Essentially, the documentation is embedded in the source code. For more information, refer to PEP-257 (*http://bit.ly/pep-257*).

```
[vagrant@master ~]$ sudo salt master.example sys.doc test.ping
test.ping:
    Used to make sure the minion is up and responding. Not an ICMP ping.
    Returns ``True``.
    CLI Example:
        salt '*' test.ping
```

 As with many examples, the preceding code is slightly edited to remove extra whitespace and blank lines. While you may see some minor formatting differences, the code snippets given should reflect the essence of what you see when you run the commands yourself. When a command runs very long and some content needs to be removed for brevity, a `<snip>` comment will be added.

The `sys.doc` function takes as its argument the name of a specific function or of an entire module. If you want to see all of the functions within the `test` module, then you can just give `sys.doc` an argument of `test`:

```
[vagrant@master ~]$ sudo salt-call sys.doc test
local:
    ----------
    test.arg:
            Print out the data passed into the function ``*args`` ...
<snip>
```

Lastly, if you want to see the documentation for all of the modules on the system, you can run `sys.doc` with no arguments at all. We should emphasize that the documentation comes from the Python code itself, not from some other set of files.

sys.list_modules, sys.list_functions: Simple Listings

The sys.doc function gives a lot of information—sometimes too much information. There are several functions aimed at giving you a higher-level view of the modules and functions available. We'll discuss two of them here. Their names should make their intended use pretty obvious:

- sys.list_modules

- sys.list_functions

As with sys.doc, both sys.list_modules and sys.list_functions take an optional argument of a module name. With no argument, all of the modules (or functions) on the minion are listed:

```
[vagrant@master ~]$ sudo salt-call sys.list_modules
local:
    - acl
    - aliases
    <snip>

[vagrant@master ~]$ sudo salt-call sys.list_functions sys
local:
    - sys.argspec
    - sys.doc
    - sys.list_functions
    - sys.list_modules
```

As with most of the modules discussed in this chapter, we have only scratched the surface of the various functions present within the sys module. In Chapter 1, we mentioned *states* and *runners*, and even quickly mentioned *returners*. There are separate functions to expose the documentation for each one of those pieces of Salt. There is even a function, sys.argspec, that will show you the various arguments and default values for each function. Learning where you can retrieve documentation will serve you well as you learn more about Salt.

cmd: Execute Via a Shell

One of the simplest and most powerful modules is cmd. While modules normally contain code that hides the exact commands run, the functions within the cmd module will *shell out* on the minion and run an arbitrary command.

 While the cmd module is very powerful, it is also very insecure. The functions within the module will run any command as root on every single minion. As a result, some places will tightly control the use of some cmd functions.

cmd.run: Run Any Command

There are several functions in the cmd module, but cmd.run is perhaps the most straightforward. It will run a command on every minion just as if you were typing it in a normal shell.

For example:

```
[vagrant@master ~]$ sudo salt \* cmd.run 'grep root /etc/passwd'
minion3.example:
    root:x:0:0:root:/root:/bin/bash
minion2.example:
    root:x:0:0:root:/root:/bin/bash
    operator:x:11:0:operator:/root:/sbin/nologin
<snip>
```

In this case, you can see the differences between a CentOS host (minion2) and an Ubuntu host (minion3).

Up until now, we have talked only about basic arguments to functions But cmd.run has a few *keyword arguments* that are worth mentioning. Adding keyword arguments to a function call is very similar to specifying keyword arguments in Python methods calls; they are just arguments where *keyword=argument*. For example, cmd.run allows you to change the current working directory using the cwd keyword argument. Let's look at the same command with and without the keyword arg:

```
[vagrant@master ~]$ sudo salt-call cmd.run 'pwd'
local:
    /root
[vagrant@master ~]$ sudo salt-call cmd.run cwd=/usr 'pwd'
local:
    /usr
```

The Salt daemons are normally run as the root user. If you need to execute a command as another user, you can use the runas argument:

```
[vagrant@master ~]$ sudo salt master\* cmd.run whoami runas=vagrant
master.example:
    vagrant
```

Another powerful keyword argument is env, which allows you to set an environment variable. The big difference with env is that it also needs to set a *key* equal to a *value*. So you need to set env=*key=value*. Obviously, that format would be very difficult to parse. In this case, you format the name and values of the environment variables as YAML and then pass that as the value to the env keyword argument:

```
[vagrant@master ~]$ sudo salt-call cmd.run env='{foo: bar}' 'echo $foo'
[INFO    ] Executing command 'echo $foo' in directory '/root'
local:
    bar
```

You will see this pattern in other functions. Just remember that Salt uses YAML at its core. When in doubt, try formatting your arguments as YAML.[2]

There is a lot more power offered by the cmd module. You should start using the various sys functions to explore all of the options available with cmd.

pkg: Manage Packages

Now that you have a solid understanding of the basic capabilities of execution modules, let's start doing some real work with our systems. One of the first things you will want to do with a system is add some packages. We have four minions, but we have not discussed how we are going to use them. As shown in Table 3-1, we are going to use minion1 and minion2 (both CentOS) as *production* servers, while we'll use minion3 and minion4 for *staging* and *development*, respectively.

Table 3-1. Minion IDs, types, and roles

Minion ID	Type	Role
minion1.example	Production (prod)	Web server
		Application server
minion2.example	Production (prod)	Database server
minion3.example	Staging (stage)	Web server
		Application server
		Database server
minion4.example	Development (dev)	Web server
		Application server
		Database server

On our web and app servers we will want to install Nginx, and on our database server we will use MySQL. As you can see in Table 3-1, in production we will want to have some separation in what our servers do. But for staging and development we want to minimize resources, so we just put everything on a single box.

---

2 Use an online YAML checker to validate your syntax. You can find a good one here: *http://yaml-online-parser.appspot.com/*.

Virtual Modules

Before we actually install Nginx on minion1, let's talk a little more about the pkg module and its functions. In our five minions (remember that the master is also a minion), we have two different operating systems, CentOS and Ubuntu, and they use different package managers. CentOS is a RedHat variant and therefore uses yum (and thus RPM), while Ubuntu uses the apt system. Both systems have their strengths and weaknesses. More importantly, to get the same information from both you need to use very different commands. But Salt keeps this all hidden from us.

Abstracting out the differences between yum and apt is what makes the pkg module so interesting. It abstracts a few different package managers into a single module, which Salt calls a *virutal module*. A virtual module is a module in name only, however; all of the code actually lives in other modules. When we discussed the sys module, we mentioned a specific function called sys.list_functions. Let's run that on a CentOS and an Ubuntu host:

```
[vagrant@master ~]$ sudo salt -L master.example,minion4.example \
  sys.list_functions pkg
master.example:
    - pkg.available_version
    - pkg.check_db
    - pkg.clean_metadata
    - pkg.del_repo
<snip>
    - pkg.upgrade_available
    - pkg.verify
    - pkg.version
minion4.example:
    - pkg.available_version
    - pkg.del_repo
<snip>
    - pkg.upgrade_available
    - pkg.version
    - pkg.version_cmp
```

Fortunately, we don't have to look at the entire list to see some differences. For the CentOS host (master), there is an additional function called pkg.check_db at the top. And the Ubuntu host (minion4) has an additional function toward the bottom named pkg.version_cmp. These differences are a result of the underlying package managers on the two different operating systems and the specific Salt modules that wrap the functionality present in each package manager.

One way of handling the differences in yum versus apt would be to hide any difference calls within the Python code itself. That is *not* what Salt does, however. Instead, Salt actually has two different Python modules: yumpkg.py and aptpkg.py. If you were to list all of the modules available on every host, you would not see either of these. That's because both modules expose their name as simply pkg. So Salt will load different Python files on each system; yumpkg.py is loaded on CentOS and aptpkg.py is loaded on Ubuntu. But, since both Python files will expose their name as pkg, other Salt utilities, like sys.doc, will know only about pkg, not yumpkg nor aptpkg. If you need to look up the specifics of the modules, either in the code or on the Web, you will need to know the full Python module name.

pkg.list_pkgs: List All Installed Packages

Let's get a list of installed packages on our systems using pkg.list_pkgs:

```
[vagrant@master ~]$ sudo salt \* pkg.list_pkgs
minion2.example:
    ----------
    MAKEDEV:
        3.24-6.el6
<snip>
minion4.example:
    ----------
    accountsservice:
        0.6.35-0ubuntu7.1
<snip>
```

These are pretty vanilla versions of each operating system. So you would expect some similarities, but a great number of differences. The preceding output is a simple list of names, each followed on the next line with the version. Again, the important thing to recognize is that while the underlying code is totally different for the two operating systems, the command you need to type is the same, and the results returned are in the same format. This abstraction is going to save us a lot of effort when we support multiple operating systems.

pkg.available_version: See What Version Will Be Installed

Now, let's use that abstraction to see what version would be installed in each host:

```
[vagrant@master ~]$ sudo salt \* pkg.available_version nginx
minion2.example:
    1.0.15-11.el6
minion1.example:
    1.0.15-11.el6
master.example:
    1.0.15-11.el6
minion3.example:
    1.4.6-1ubuntu3.1
minion4.example:
    1.4.6-1ubuntu3.1
```

The preceding output should not come as a surprise. The different package systems have different nuances when it comes to releases. So it is not uncommon to see different versions of the same software on the different operating systems. Now that we have seen which version will be installed, let's install Nginx on one of our hosts.

pkg.install: Install Packages

Let's install Nginx on a single host: `minion1`. This is the first of several hosts we will configure over the course of the book:

```
[vagrant@master ~]$ sudo salt minion1.example pkg.install nginx
minion1.example:
    ----------
    GeoIP:
        ----------
        new:
            1.5.1-5.el6
        old:
<snip>
    nginx:
        ----------
        new:
            1.0.15-11.el6
        old:
<snip>
```

One of the first things you'll notice is that there is a lot of output. When the Nginx package was installed, the package manager (in this case, yum) also installed all of the dependencies. Also, both the old and new versions are shown to indicate to the user the current state as well as the previous one. (When `pkg.install` installs a brand new package and there is no old version, then the old version is simply reported as the empty string.)

Now, that the Nginx package is installed, we can use the `version` function to validate:

```
[vagrant@master ~]$ sudo salt minion1.example pkg.version nginx
minion1.example:
    1.0.15-11.el6
```

The `pkg` module will allow you to manage your packages in a consistent manner across all of your hosts, regardless of the underlying operating system. It uses the power of a virtual module to appear under the same name for many different systems. But the exact functionality is different for different types of systems.

user: Manage Users

The next step of our system configuration is adding a couple of users. Earlier we mentioned our systems and what roles they will play in the final architecture. Let's look at our users in Table 3-2.

Table 3-2. User logins, names, and roles

Login	Name	Role
wilma	Wilma Flintstone	DBA
fred	Fred Flintstone	Developer
barney	Barney Rubble	Developer and QA
betty	Betty Rubble	Developer and QA

All of the developers will need access to the *dev* hosts, the QA engineers will need access to the *qa* host, and the DBA (database administration) needs access to all hosts within a database.

user.add: Add Users

As before, we will just add a single user to show how you can use the execution modules to manually configure your systems. The other users will be saved for the following chapter when we introduce a higher-level abstraction, namely states.

The user module has several very straightforward functions for managing users. Let's add a single user using user.add. We will focus on the *prod* hosts first:

```
[vagrant@master ~]$ sudo salt minion2.example user.add wilma
minion2.example:
    True
```

Let's verify using the cmd.run example from earlier:

```
[vagrant@master ~]$ sudo salt minion2.example cmd.run 'grep wilma /etc/passwd'
minion2.example:
    wilma:x:501:501::/home/wilma:/bin/bash
```

Next, we will use another user function to verify without using cmd.run.

user.list_users, user.info: Get User Info

Rather than using cmd.run, which can cause problems if you happen to make an unfortunate typo with the command, we can verify using users.list_users:

```
[vagrant@master ~]$ sudo salt minion2.example user.list_users
minion2.example:
    - adm
<snip>
    - wilma
```

This list is great, but it doesn't provide as much information as earlier when we parsed the password file. We can use user.info to get additional information about a user:

```
[vagrant@master ~]$ sudo salt minion2.example user.info wilma
minion2.example:
    ----------
    fullname:

    gid:
        501
    groups:
        - wilma
    home:
        /home/wilma
    homephone:

    name:
        wilma
    passwd:
        x
    roomnumber:

    shell:
        /bin/bash
    uid:
        501
    workphone:
```

It should be noted that under the hood, Salt uses the basic system utilities. In the case with user.add, it uses the useradd command-line application available on both CentOS and Ubuntu. When we added our user earlier, we specified only the login, wilma. The rest of the defaults came from the useradd utility, not the Salt module. You will see this frequently with Salt: it uses various system utilities wrapped inside Salt code. These utilities have their own defaults, which affects Salt as well.

There are a number of additional features in the user module. Please explore and play with the different options. We will come back to user management in Chapters 4 and 5.

saltutil: Access Various Salt Utilities

We could spend the entire book discussing the various execution modules and what they do. The previous coverage should be a good example of what Salt can do. There are many modules and functions that will ease some common tasks. But what about Salt itself? There is a module that contains several important utilities specific to Salt. Unsurprisingly, it's named saltutil.

With most modules, it's best to have a high-level understanding of what they do and then learn more about them when you run across a specific need. The saltutil functions are a little different because they help you manage Salt itself, rather than managing your systems. saltutil contains functions to help manage jobs, manage keys, and update various parts of the system. Unfortunately, we cannot cover all of the functions in the saltutil module since that would require concepts we haven't discussed yet. But, along with the sys module, saltutil has a number of functions that will prove very handy.

Salt does its best to update any pieces that you need. But there are times when you can't wait for Salt or you need something specific updated. There are several functions that can help:

```
[vagrant@master ~]$ sudo salt-call sys.list_functions saltutil | grep sync
    - saltutil.sync_all
    - saltutil.sync_grains
    - saltutil.sync_modules
    - saltutil.sync_outputters
    - saltutil.sync_renderers
    - saltutil.sync_returners
    - saltutil.sync_states
    - saltutil.sync_utils
```

Many of those names should look familiar (e.g., grains and returners), but we have discussed them only briefly. The saltutil.sync_modules pertains directly to this chapter. We don't have anything to update right now, but let's run it to see what it outputs:

```
[vagrant@master ~]$ sudo salt master.example saltutil.sync_modules
master.example:
```

Not every exciting. But if we look at saltutil.sync_all, we can get a better view of what is happening:

```
[vagrant@master ~]$ sudo salt master.example saltutil.sync_all
master.example:
    ----------
    grains:
    modules:
    outputters:
    renderers:
    returners:
    states:
    utils:
```

This simply calls *all* of the other sync functions. If something had changed, you would have seen some specifics in each section. For example, if we had updated a module, then right below modules: there would be a list of the specific modules that were updated on that minion.

The job management routines will require a little more work to play with. Open a second window on the master and execute a long-running command:

```
[vagrant@master ~]$ sudo salt master.example cmd.run 'sleep 100'
```

In the other window, we can look for the preceding job using the `saltutil.running` function:

```
[vagrant@master ~]$ sudo salt master.example saltutil.running
master.example:
    |_
      ----------
      arg:
          - sleep 100
      fun:
          cmd.run
      jid:
          20150127040117547273
          sudo_vagrant
<snip>
```

We have cut out some of the details, but the parts most relevant to Salt are shown. This function allows you to get a little more information about what is running on a minion. If the preceding job kept running, we could use the `saltutil.kill_job` function. Let's start a new job, find the job ID, and then kill that job:

```
[vagrant@master ~]$  sudo salt master.example cmd.run 'sleep 100'

[vagrant@master ~]$ sudo salt master.example saltutil.running
master.example:
    |_
      ----------
      arg:
          - sleep 100
      fun:
          cmd.run
      jid:
          20150127040542908007
      pid:
          1006
      ret:

      tgt:
          master.example
      tgt_type:
          glob
      user:
          sudo_vagrant

[vagrant@master ~]$ sudo salt master.example saltutil.kill_job 20150127040542908007
master.example:
    Signal 9 sent to job 20150127040542908007 at pid 1006
```

Again, we encourage you to view the documentation online to keep up with changes with all of the execution modules. But it will serve you well to become very familiar with all of the functions within `saltutil`. Many more of the functions will make sense after you've finished reading the entire book. We need to introduce more of Salt's basic functionality before explaining some of those functions.

Summary

Execution modules are great and allow you to interact with many systems at once. They also abstract out many of the differences in your systems, like how the `pkg` module will interact with both CentOS's yum package manager and Ubuntu's apt. But they still require you to explicitly enter all of the commands every time you want to run them. Next we will introduce the *state system*. It will give you the power to specify a recipe, or state, for a set of systems and then just *apply* that given recipe to perform the desired action.

CHAPTER 4

Configuration Management: Salt States

The remote execution framework provides the basis for a number of higher-level abstractions. Running remote commands on a number of minions is great. But when you add another web server or another database server, hopefully that new server will have something in common with other servers. Reusing components helps maintain a base level of consistency in your environment. Salt provides a simple but powerful file format that allows you to specify a desired recipe, or *state*, describing how you want a host to look, and then you simply apply that state. The states can be combined so you can build on simple pieces to make more complicated states.

 You can find the complete list of state modules on the SaltStack website (*http://bit.ly/builtin_state_mods*).

State File Overview

You describe a state via Salt state (SLS) files. As with most of Salt's core, the most basic format is YAML. One of the big advantages of YAML is that it is language-agnostic; it is just a data format. The format of the states uses standard data structure constructs:

- Strings
- Numbers
- Arrays (lists)
- Hashes (dictionaries)

It is important to remember that YAML is just a simple representation of the data structure. You can alter the underlying file format if you use a different *renderer*.

SLS Example: Adding a User

In the previous chapter, we added a single user on a host. But we want this user, and the rest of the users, to be added automatically every time we add another machine. Let's handle just the `wilma` user for the moment. Here's a very simple SLS file to add the `wilma` user:

```
user_wilma:
  user.present:
    - name: wilma
    - fullname: Wilma Flintstone
    - uid: 2001
    - home: /home/wilma
```

We are using the same basic information as before, and we have added a little more. We are using the *state module* called `user` and the function `present`. In the previous chapter, we discussed execution modules. Now, we are instead using state modules. They often look very similar and sometimes have the same arguments, but they are different. When we added a user, we used the `user.add` execution function. Now, we want to make sure the user exists using the `user.present` state function. At their core, state modules rely on execution modules to actually make the changes needed, but state modules will add further functionality on top of that. In the case of `user.present`, we only want to call the execution function `user.add` if we really need to add that user. If the user already exists, then we can skip it. Since there is a logical difference between running an add user command versus *running an add user command if the user is missing*, the function names may be different. The user state module, like other state modules, will make a change only if it detects there is a delta between the real state and the desired state. The side effect is that you can run a state over and over again, and as long as there is no delta, nothing will change. In other words, state calls are *idempotent*.

SLS format and state documentation

Let's explore the format of the SLS file for a moment. As we said, it is a standard YAML-formatted file. The first line is an ID that can be referenced in other state files or later in the file. We will use the state IDs heavily when we order states in "State Ordering" on page 58.

Next is the command or *state declaration*. In the previous chapter, we talked about using `sys.doc` to look at the documentation for a given module. But execution functions and state functions are not the same. Fortunately, there is another `sys` function that can help us out: `sys.state_doc`:

```
[vagrant@master ~]$ sudo salt-call sys.state_doc user.present
local:
    ----------
    user:
        Management of user accounts
        ============================
        The user module is used to create and manage user settings, users can be
        set as either absent or present
<snip>
```

If you run the preceding command, you will see the rest of the options. Those options are what appear next in the state file. In our specific case, this includes options for the full name, the user ID (`uid`), and the home directory.

One last thing we should mention: the first argument, `name`, can be used as the ID of the state itself. So we can rewrite the preceding state as the following:

```
wilma:
  user.present:
    - fullname: Wilma Flintstone
    - uid: 2001
    - home: /home/wilma
```

In this case, it is implied that the name (aka login) of the user is the same as the ID of the state itself. This can be very handy and can simplify your states a little. However, these state names can be referenced elsewhere and may cause more confusion than it's worth. With usernames, it isn't quite as obvious as with, say, names of packages. So be aware of this shortcut, but use it with caution.

When we introduced `sys.doc`, we also mentioned `sys.list_modules` and `sys.list_functions`. There are corresponding calls for state modules and functions: `sys.list_state_modules` and `sys.list_state_functions`:

```
[vagrant@master ~]$ sudo salt-call sys.list_state_modules
local:
    - alias
<snip>
    - user
<snip>

[vagrant@master ~]$ sudo salt-call sys.list_state_functions user
local:
    - user.absent
    - user.present
```

Explore the various state functions within the `sys` module to become more familiar with the large list of state modules available within Salt.

Setting the file roots

The state file is great, but what do we do with it? The first thing we need to do is tell the Salt master where to find the files. In Salt's terms, we need to set up the file server. We have mentioned the master configuration file: */etc/salt/master*. We could easily edit that file, but we could also create some smaller files in a directory: */etc/salt/master.d*. The main configuration file is a bit large and unwieldy, but the default configuration has an include statement that will grab all of the files matching */etc/salt/master.d/*.conf*:

```
[vagrant@master ~]$ sudo grep default_include /etc/salt/master
#default_include: master.d/*.conf
```

(The master config file has many of the defaults listed, but they've been commented out just to highlight what the default settings are.)

```
[vagrant@master ~]$ sudo cat /etc/salt/master.d/file-roots.conf
file_roots:
  base:
  - /srv/salt/file/base
```

Add that file and then restart the Salt master:

```
[vagrant@master ~]$ sudo service salt-master restart
Stopping salt-master daemon:                               [  OK  ]
Starting salt-master daemon:                               [  OK  ]
```

When we introduced the saltutil execution module, we demonstrated syncing from the master to a minion. For many of the files synced, the *file_roots* configuration option specifies the directory where you can find them. Salt has a small built-in file server that copies any necessary files between hosts. This file server communicates over the standard ZeroMQ channels that the rest of Salt uses, so the files are transferred securely and without any additional configuration.

Salt can partition minions into overlapping groups called *environments*. Right now, we are concerned only with the *base* environment, indicated by the base keyword.

Executing a state file

We have set up our Salt master with our *file_roots* directory, which is necessary for using states. We will add the preceding example state definition to a file inside *file_roots*:

```
[vagrant@master ~]$ cat /srv/salt/file/base/user-wilma.sls
user_wilma:
  user.present:
  - name: wilma
  - fullname: Wilma Flintstone
  - uid: 2001
  - home: /home/wilma
```

Now we will introduce the `state` execution module.

These terms may be getting a little confusing. There are many state modules, such as `pkg` and `user`. There are also many execution modules, such as `cmd` and `sys`. But, in order to execute states, you need to run something (i.e., an execution module). As a result, there is an execution module called `state`. This is how you *run* state modules, but `state` itself is *not* a state module. If this doesn't make sense, hopefully it will after you use Salt for a while.

As with all Salt commands, we can use `sys.doc` to get an idea of `state`'s capabilities. The first function we will introduce is `state.show_sls`:

```
[vagrant@master ~]$ sudo salt master.example state.show_sls user-wilma
master.example:
    ----------
    user_wilma:
        ----------
        __env__:
            base
        __sls__:
            user-wilma
        user:
            |_
              ----------
              name:
                  wilma
            |_
              ----------
              fullname:
                  Wilma Flintstone
            |_
              ----------
              uid:
                  2001
            |_
              ----------
              home:
                  /home/wilma
            - present
            |_
              ----------
              order:
                  10000
```

This shows the basic data structure Salt uses after reading the file. Most of it should look pretty familiar. You can see all of the various arguments to `user.present`, as well as the declaration of the `state` function itself, albeit broken into a couple of different lines. There is the reference to the `user` state module toward the top. But the specific function, `present`, is given at the bottom. What is important to recognize is that the module (`user`), and the specific function (`present`), are joined in the original state file, but Salt pulls them apart when parsing the file. We won't be using that fact in this book, but it's worth noting.

 I (Craig) use state.show_sls almost every day. I use it to verify and debug almost every state (SLS file) I write. It is extremely handy to see how Salt parses the SLS file and if it matches everything I expect. Many simple syntax errors, including common YAML errors, will be caught by state.show_sls, without affecting any minions. So it is a very handy tool that you should learn.

We can run this state against minion2 and we should see very little change since we already added that user. To execute the state, we simply call state.sls:

```
[vagrant@master ~]$ sudo salt minion2.example state.sls user-wilma
minion2.example:
  ----------
            ID: user_wilma
      Function: user.present
          Name: wilma
        Result: True
       Comment: Updated user wilma
       Started: 06:16:52.541678
      Duration: 193.926 ms
       Changes:
                ----------
                fullname:
                    Wilma Flintstone
                uid:
                    2001

Summary
------------
Succeeded: 1 (changed=1)
Failed:    0
------------
Total states run:     1
```

The important thing to notice is that after the state is applied, Salt will show you what changed. In this example, some of the user data already existed. But the fullname and the uid did change and Salt reported those details. If we run this once again, we should see no change this time:

```
[vagrant@master ~]$ sudo salt minion2.example state.sls user-wilma
minion2.example:
  ----------
            ID: user_wilma
      Function: user.present
          Name: wilma
        Result: True
       Comment: User wilma is present and up to date
```

```
        Started: 06:19:32.235330
       Duration: 1.599 ms
        Changes:

Summary
-----------
Succeeded: 1
Failed:    0
-----------
Total states run:    1
```

This time the `Changes:` section is empty, indicating that nothing changed. This is very handy; we should be able to run this state many times without any undesirable changes. We will take advantage of this fact later using something called a *highstate*, which is a collection of states that, all together, form our complete definition of a host.

Working with the Multilayered State System

We have discussed repeatedly how the different pieces of Salt build on top of each other to present a great deal of functionality to the user. Even within each piece there can be multiple layers that allow the advanced user a great deal of flexibility and power, and also provide a newcomer sufficient power to get complex tasks done easily.

The state system is no exception.

state.single: Calling a state using data on the command line

At the very bottommost layer are the function calls themselves. They are similar to the execution modules, but they are distinct.

We can call the state functions directly by using the `state.single` execution module:

```
[vagrant@master ~]$ sudo salt minion2.example state.single user.present \
name=wilma fullname='Wilma Flintstone' uid=2001 home=/home/wilma
minion2.example:
  ---------
          ID: wilma
    Function: user.present
      Result: True
     Comment: User wilma is present and up to date
     Started: 06:25:18.704908
    Duration: 1.646 ms
     Changes:

Summary
-----------
Succeeded: 1
Failed:    0
```

```
          ----------
          Total states run:      1
```

This call to `state.single` says to execute the `user.present` state function in the same way that we specified the state in the state file, */srv/salt/file/base/user-wilma.sls*. The arguments are the same between the two. This can come in handy when, say, you're testing state functions.

 Notice how the ID is missing from the `state.single` call. Since this is a one-time call and only one state module is used, there is no reason to give it a unique ID.

The returned data is exactly the same as what we saw earlier when we used the SLS file:

```
sudo salt minion2.example state.sls user-wilma
```

Namely, the user is already present, so no action was taken.

state.low: States with raw data

As we progress up (or down, if you prefer) the state layers, we get further away from the familiar data format we saw in the SLS file. The next layer is called the *low chunk*. At this layer, the state is completely abstracted out as data. We mentioned that the state function we called, `user.present`, is actually a combination of two pieces that are just conveniently joined. When we call the low chunk, we see how that is represented by different parts of the data structure:

```
[vagrant@master ~]$ sudo salt minion2.example state.low \
        '{state: user, fun: present, name: wilma}'
minion2.example:
    ----------
    __run_num__:
        0
    changes:
        ----------
    comment:
        User wilma is present and up to date
    duration:
        1.785
    name:
        wilma
    result:
        True
    start_time:
        06:34:50.250740
```

In this call, we specify the state (user) and the function (present) as two different parts of the data structure. You can view this data for an existing SLS file by using state.show_low_sls.

 A few arguments were simply left off for brevity. You can specify all of the same arguments using state.low.

Hopefully, you won't need to dig this deep into states when building your own systems. But this functional foundation may prove useful when you get stuck and cannot figure out what is happening with your states; you can start peering down into the rabbit hole. Next, we will go in the opposite direction and talk about higher-level abstractions that allow us to build a complete host recipe.

Highstate and the Top File

Now that we've gone into the low levels of the state system, we want to look at the real power that lies with combining states. The example we have used until now has just been one file, and we have called it directly using state.sls. But this is not the power we are referring to. We want to be able to add a new host, annotate it (as, say, a web server), and then just have all of the right packages installed, users set up, and so on. Essentially, we want the correct *recipe* applied to the given host. This means not only combining many states together, but also knowing which combination to run on which machine. The highstate layer is used to combine various states together. We will discuss that next when we introduce the top file.

The Top File

We want to combine states into more complex highstates. The file that defines this state is called the top file and it normally named *top.sls*. It appears in the *file_roots* directory. When we set up *file_roots*, we mentioned the base environment. The top file goes into this environment. We start with a very simple top file that executes our state to add the wilma user:

```
[vagrant@master ~]$ cat /srv/salt/file/base/top.sls
base:
  'minion2.example':
  - user-wilma
```

At the highest level in the top file is the environment. So far, we have dealt only with a single environment: base. In order to keep things simple, we will continue to use only base for a while.

Next, you have the targeted minion. In this case, we want only the state, user-wilma, added to a single minion. But, in the general case, in each environment you give a list of targets. This targeting is exactly the same as what we saw in Chapter 2. But, just as with the single environment, let's keep it simple for now and focus only on minion IDs.

We can view the effective top file for any minion using the state.show_top command:

```
[vagrant@master ~]$ sudo salt minion2.example state.show_top
minion2.example:
    ----------
    base:
        - user-wilma
```

The output shows how the top file would be generated for that specific minion, minion2. For another example, let's try running against another minion:

```
[vagrant@master ~]$ sudo salt master.example state.show_top
master.example:
    ----------
```

In this case, the top file is shown as empty because there is only a single target and it doesn't apply to master.example.

Before adding the rest of the users, let's suppose we want to add the vim package on every host. We will use the pkg.installed state function, but this time we will put the file into a subdirectory to give us a little more structure in our file layout. Since we are going to install the package on every host, we will simply call the directory *default* and the file *packages.sls*:

```
[vagrant@master ~]$ cat /srv/salt/file/base/default/packages.sls
packages_vim:
  pkg.installed:
    - name: vim
```

Then let's add it for every host (*) in our modified top file:

```
[vagrant@master ~]$ cat /srv/salt/file/base/top.sls
base:
  '*':
    - default.packages

  'minion2.example':
    - user-wilma
```

Directories are not denoted with slashes, but with dots. So, a state directory of *a/b/c/d* would be given as *a.b.c.d* in the *top_file*.

Since we have a more interesting top file, we can start to discuss executing a highstate. Since a highstate execution references the top file, there is no need to specify any arguments. The target given in the top file will create a unique run on every minion.

If we run it, we see a problem:

```
[vagrant@master ~]$ sudo salt \* state.highstate
minion2.example:
  ----------
            ID: packages_vim
      Function: pkg.installed
          Name: vim
        Result: False
       Comment: Package 'vim' not found (possible matches: vim-enhanced)
       Started: 08:05:40.253299
      Duration: 22321.085 ms
       Changes:
  ----------
            ID: user_wilma
      Function: user.present
          Name: wilma
        Result: True
       Comment: User wilma is present and up to date
       Started: 08:06:02.574640
      Duration: 5.033 ms
       Changes:

Summary
-----------
Succeeded: 1
Failed:    1
-----------
Total states run:     2
minion3.example:
  ----------
            ID: packages_vim
      Function: pkg.installed
          Name: vim
        Result: True
       Comment: Package vim is already installed.
       Started: 08:05:57.273826
      Duration: 10550.292 ms
       Changes:

Summary
-----------
Succeeded: 1
Failed:    0
-----------
Total states run:     1
```

We have two different operating systems that call the vim package different things. It installed fine on the Ubuntu hosts, but CentOS needs us to install the vim-enhanced package. We can adjust things slightly to handle this for now, which means breaking up the *all hosts* (*) target. We mentioned the concept of grains back in Chapter 2, and we briefly explored target using grains. We can definitely use this concept within the top file:[1]

```
[vagrant@master ~]$ cat /srv/salt/file/base/top.sls
base:
  'os:CentOS':
    - match: grain
    - default.vim-enhanced

  'os:Ubuntu':
    - match: grain
    - default.vim

  'minion2.example':
    - user-wilma
```

Next we create two new files: *vim.sls* and *vim-enhanced.sls*. (You may as well delete the old *packages.sls*; we won't reference it, but we will come back to it in Chapter 5.)

```
[vagrant@master ~]$ cat /srv/salt/file/base/default/vim.sls
packages_vim:
  pkg.installed:
    - name: vim
[vagrant@master ~]$ cat /srv/salt/file/base/default/vim-enhanced.sls
packages_vim:
  pkg.installed:
    - name: vim-enhanced
```

We can rerun our `state.highstate` and we should see everything run without any more issues:

```
[vagrant@master ~]$ sudo salt \* state.highstate
minion3.example:
    ---------
          ID: packages_vim
    Function: pkg.installed
        Name: vim
      Result: True
     Comment: Package vim is already installed.
     Started: 01:28:47.448266
    Duration: 705.834 ms
     Changes:
```

---

1 As of Salt 2014.7, the compound matcher is the default in the top file. The example shown is still accurate, but we can make it simpler by using a target of `G@os:CentOS` and then removing the `match` line.

```
Summary
-----------
Succeeded: 1
Failed:    0
-----------
Total states run:     1
minion4.example:
---------
          ID: packages_vim
    Function: pkg.installed
        Name: vim
      Result: True
     Comment: Package vim is already installed.
<snip>
```

We have a package installed on every host, with some minor differences on our two operating systems. We should return to our users and get all of them installed. Table 3-1 listed our minions with their roles, and Table 3-2 listed the users with their roles. When we combine them, we should get the list of users to add to every host, as shown in Table 4-1.

Table 4-1. Minion IDs and corresponding users

Minion ID	Users
minion2	wilma
minion3	wilma, barney, betty
minion4	wilma, barney, betty, fred

We can use this to create more structure for the users, as well. We'll create a users directory and put our files there. Also, we'll create a file for each user, a file for both QA users (barney and betty), and a file with all of the users. Since we are creating some more structure with the users, let's also remove the specific call to add wilma directly. Rather, let's add all of the DBAs. The include statement will make this easy.

Let's look at the top file:

```
[vagrant@master ~]$ cat /srv/salt/file/base/top.sls
base:
  'os:CentOS':
    - match: grain
    - default.vim-enhanced

  'os:Ubuntu':
    - match: grain
    - default.vim

  'minion2.example':
```

```
      - users.dba

    'minion3.example':
      - users.dba
      - users.qa

    'minion4.example':
      - users.all
```

The top file is really taking shape. We do have to individually specify the minion IDs, but we will fix that later.

We will create a state file for each user we want to add. This will give us the necessary flexibility in where we install the users. (We will group them in just a moment.)

```
[vagrant@master ~]$ cat /srv/salt/file/base/users/{wilma,fred,barney,betty}.sls
user_wilma:
  user.present:
  - name: wilma
  - fullname: Wilma Flintstone
  - uid: 2001
user_fred:
  user.present:
  - name: fred
  - fullname: Fred Flintstone
  - uid: 2002
user_barney:
  user.present:
  - name: barney
  - fullname: Barney Rubble
  - uid: 2003
user_betty:
  user.present:
  - name: betty
  - fullname: Betty Rubble
  - uid: 2004
```

(We removed the home directory. We just don't need it any longer.)

Next, we have the *grouped* user files utilizing `include` statements:

```
[vagrant@master ~]$ cat /srv/salt/file/base/users/dba.sls
include:
- users.wilma
[vagrant@master ~]$ cat /srv/salt/file/base/users/qa.sls
include:
- users.barney
- users.betty
```

This is simple enough. Just as with the top file, directories are separated with dots, not slashes. One thing to note: all files included are referenced from a file root. Since we have only the single directory defined in *file_roots*, all state files must be specified relative to that single directory: */srv/salt/file/base*. This can be a little tedious, especially if we continue to create more subdirectories. There is a shorthand: you can refer to state files in *your current directory* simply with a leading dot. Let's use that shorthand with the *all users* state:

```
[vagrant@master ~]$ cat /srv/salt/file/base/users/all.sls
include:
- .fred
- .wilma
- .barney
- .betty
```

 You can use the cp.list_states execution function to see how Salt sees the various states and represents them.

With a more complex top file, we can use state.show_top for a specific minion to make sure it looks as we expect:

```
[vagrant@master ~]$ sudo salt minion3.example state.show_top
minion3.example:
    ----------
    base:
        - default.vim
        - users.dba
        - users.qa
```

Now that we have a top file that looks good, we can simply run a highstate (state.highstate) against all of the minions, and the correct users and packages will get installed on every host:

```
[vagrant@master ~]$ sudo salt '*' state.highstate
minion2.example:
    ---------
              ID: packages_vim
        Function: pkg.installed
            Name: vim-enhanced
          Result: True
         Comment: Package vim-enhanced is already installed.
         Started: 01:37:18.806663
        Duration: 878.505 ms
         Changes:
    ---------
              ID: user_wilma
        Function: user.present
            Name: wilma
          Result: True
         Comment: User wilma is present and up to date
         Started: 01:37:19.685347
        Duration: 1.774 ms
```

```
        Changes:

    Summary
    ----------
    Succeeded: 2
    Failed:    0
    ----------
    Total states run:    2
    minion3.example:
    ---------
    <snip>
```

When we were running individual states, we used `state.show_sls` to show the lower-level state data structure. There is an analogous command for highstates: `state.show_highstate`:

```
    [vagrant@master ~]$ sudo salt minion4.example state.show_highstate
    minion4.example:
        ----------
        packages_vim:
            ----------
            __env__:
                base
            __sls__:
                default.vim
            pkg:
                |_
                  ----------
                  name:
                      vim
                - installed
                |_
                  ----------
                  order:
                      10000
    <snip>
```

As you can see, the high-level declarations given in *top.sls* and the referenced state files are broken down into a Salt data structure. However, there is an added element: `order`. When you are running multiple states, the order in which they execute can be important. The states are ordered using a simple numeric sort. If you need to force an order in your states, there are a couple of options.

State Ordering

When you compile the states for highstate, the states will always be ordered and repeatable. However, the order that Salt generates may not be what you need. The `require` declaration will force a specific state to be executed before a given state. And there is also a way to watch another state and then execute code based on any changes. Lastly, you can peer into the future with `prereq`, which will look at other states to see if they will change. If they are going to change, then run the referencing state.

require: Depend on Another State

As we mentioned, there are many times when you need to ensure that one action happens before another. The `require` declaration will enforce that the named state executes before the current state. For example, if state A has a `require` for state B, then state B will always run before state A.

Before we get to the details of a `require`, let's go back to the Nginx package we installed manually in the previous chapter using the `pkg.install` execution function.

We can verify the package using the `pkg.version` execution function:

```
[vagrant@master ~]$ sudo salt minion1\* pkg.version nginx
minion1.example:
    1.0.15-11.el6
```

Let's now add a state to automatically install the Nginx package on `minion1`. Earlier, when we discussed our five example minions, we gave each one a role. We are going to add a little more structure to *file_roots* by adding a *roles* directory and then a *webserver* subdirectory:

```
[vagrant@master ~]$ cat /srv/salt/file/base/roles/webserver/packages.sls
roles_webserver_packages:
  pkg.installed:
  - name: nginx
```

We will also need to make sure the Nginx service is running:

```
[vagrant@master ~]$ cat /srv/salt/file/base/roles/webserver/start.sls
roles_webserver_start:
  service.running:
  - name: nginx
  - require:
    - pkg: nginx
```

As you can see, before we can actually start the Nginx service, we need to make sure that the Nginx package exists. The `require` declaration takes a list of dictionaries. The key of the dictionary is the name of the state module—in this case, pkg—and then the value of the dictionary is the name of the state. Remember, in this context it is the state's name (nginx), *not* the ID (roles_webserver_packages).

Now we have to add these states to the top file. We could easily just add both of them to the `minion1.example` target. However, there is another shortcut: `init.sls`.

init.sls directory shortcut

We have referred to individual states using their filenames, minus the *sls* extension. However, we have not discussed how to reference a *directory* instead of an individual file. If there is a file named *init.sls* in a directory, then you can simply reference the directory name without *init.sls*.

If we continue our previous example, we can add *webserver/roles/init.sls* and then reference it in the top file:

```
[vagrant@master ~]$ cat /srv/salt/file/base/roles/webserver/init.sls
include:
- users.www
- .packages
- .start
[vagrant@master ~]$ cat /srv/salt/file/base/top.sls
base:
  'os:CentOS':
    - match: grain
    - default.vim-enhanced

  'os:Ubuntu':
    - match: grain
    - default.vim

  'minion1.example':
    - roles.webserver

  'minion2.example':
    - users.dba

  'minion3.example':
    - users.dba
    - users.qa

  'minion4.example':
    - users.all
```

The file *roles/webserver/init.sls* also makes use of the leading dot shorthand to reference files within the current directory. In our new top file, we have added a target for `minion1.example` and added a single state: `roles.webserver`. We also included another state, `users/www.sls`:

```
[vagrant@master ~]$ cat /srv/salt/file/base/users/www.sls
user_www:
  user.present:
  - name: www
  - fullname: WebServer User
  - uid: 5001
```

As you can see, we can include any file into another state. We simply have to reference it based off the main file root. We can now run a highstate on `minion1`:

```
[vagrant@master ~]$ sudo salt minion1\* state.highstate
minion1.example:
    ----------
          ID: packages_vim
    Function: pkg.installed
<snip>
    ----------
          ID: user_www
    Function: user.present
<snip>
    ----------
          ID: roles_webserver_packages
    Function: pkg.installed
<snip>
    ----------
          ID: roles_webserver_start
    Function: service.running
        Name: nginx
      Result: True
     Comment: Started Service nginx
     Started: 02:14:13.267952
    Duration: 371.647 ms
     Changes:
              ----------
              nginx:
                  True

Summary
    ----------
Succeeded: 4 (changed=1)
Failed:    0
    ----------
Total states run:    4
```

Most of the output should look familiar. We have left in the entire output from the
`roles_webserver_start` state. As you can see, it reported back some changes (specifically, that the service was started up). The important part to note is that the package
was verified before the service was started. While in a setup this small you may be
able to skip the `require`, there will come a time when you will have to ensure that one
state runs before another. Next, we will talk about how to execute an additional action
only if another state reports a change.

watch: Run Based on Other Changes

Often when you deploy a new version of an application, you will need to restart the
application to pick up these changes. The `watch` statement will execute additional
states if any change is detected. We are going to create a fake website consisting of a
single file. (You can easily extrapolate this idea to a package with many configuration
files.) We are going to add another state: `sites`:

```
[vagrant@master ~]$ cat /srv/salt/file/base/sites/init.sls
sites_first:
  file.managed:
  - name: /usr/share/nginx/html/first.html
  - source: salt://sites/src/first.html
  - user: www
  - mode: 0644
  service.running:
  - name: nginx
  - watch:
      - file: /usr/share/nginx/html/first.html
```

And the single file we are going to manage:

```
[vagrant@master ~]$ cat /srv/salt/file/base/sites/src/first.html
<html>
<head><title>First Site</title></head>
<body>
<h3>First Site</h3>
</body></html>
```

Last, we need to add this new state to the top file so that the given host(s) will always have it applied on a highstate:

```
[vagrant@master ~]$ cat /srv/salt/file/base/top.sls
base:
  'os:CentOS':
    - match: grain
    - default.vim-enhanced

  'os:Ubuntu':
    - match: grain
    - default.vim

  'minion1.example':
    - roles.webserver
    - sites

  'minion2.example':
    - users.dba

  'minion3.example':
    - users.dba
    - users.qa

  'minion4.example':
    - users.all
```

As you can see, we have added this state only to minion1 for the moment. We need to execute a highstate on this host to get the new site (aka file) onto that host. Before we actually run this new state, let's discuss a way to test states using test=true. You can add an argument of test=true to various state functions—most notably, state.sls and `state.highstate`. Before we run our highstate, let's look at the new `site` state and what happens when we add the `test` flag:

```
[vagrant@master ~]$ sudo salt minion1.example state.sls sites test=true
minion1.example:
  ----------
            ID: sites_first
      Function: file.managed
          Name: /usr/share/nginx/html/first.html
        Result: None
       Comment: The file /usr/share/nginx/html/first.html is set to be changed
       Started: 21:59:40.821641
      Duration: 243.354 ms
       Changes:
                ----------
                newfile:
                    /usr/share/nginx/html/first.html
  ----------
            ID: sites_first
      Function: service.running
          Name: nginx
        Result: None
       Comment: Service is set to be restarted
       Started: 21:59:41.093111
      Duration: 25.794 ms
       Changes:

Summary
----------
Succeeded: 2 (unchanged=2, changed=1)
Failed:    0
----------
Total states run:     2
```

> The `test=true` flag is very handy for debugging any issues you may see with state ordering.

Running a highstate with the same flag will give very similar results:

```
[vagrant@master ~]$ sudo salt minion1.example state.highstate test=true
minion1.example:
  ----------
            ID: packages_vim
      Function: pkg.installed
          Name: vim-enhanced
        Result: True
       Comment: Package vim-enhanced is already installed.
       Started: 22:04:16.955372
```

```
        Duration: 786.249 ms
         Changes:
<snip>
  ---------
           ID: sites_first
     Function: file.managed
         Name: /usr/share/nginx/html/first.html
       Result: None
      Comment: The file /usr/share/nginx/html/first.html is set to be changed
      Started: 22:04:17.774924
     Duration: 4.676 ms
      Changes:
                ----------
                newfile:
                    /usr/share/nginx/html/first.html
  ---------
           ID: sites_first
     Function: service.running
         Name: nginx
       Result: None
      Comment: Service is set to be restarted
      Started: 22:04:17.807615
     Duration: 26.997 ms
      Changes:

Summary
-----------
Succeeded: 6 (unchanged=2, changed=1)
Failed:    0
-----------
Total states run:    6
```

Now, we simply run the highstate without the test flag and have our new site deployed:

```
[vagrant@master ~]$ sudo salt minion1.example state.highstate
minion1.example:
<snip>
  ---------
           ID: roles_webserver_start
     Function: service.running
         Name: nginx
       Result: True
      Comment: The service nginx is already running
      Started: 22:06:47.380502
     Duration: 27.698 ms
      Changes:
  ---------
           ID: sites_first
     Function: file.managed
         Name: /usr/share/nginx/html/first.html
       Result: True
      Comment: File /usr/share/nginx/html/first.html updated
```

```
    Started: 22:06:47.409228
   Duration: 290.492 ms
    Changes:
                ----------
                diff:
                    New file
                mode:
                    0644
                user:
                    www
----------
          ID: sites_first
    Function: service.running
        Name: nginx
      Result: True
     Comment: Service restarted
     Started: 22:06:47.731534
    Duration: 337.565 ms
     Changes:
                ----------
                nginx:
                    True

Summary
----------
Succeeded: 6 (changed=2)
Failed:    0
----------
Total states run:    6
```

We can now do a simple test to verify the site is working:

```
[vagrant@master ~]$ curl 172.31.0.21/first.html
<html>
<head><title>First Site</title></head>
<body>
<h3>First Site</h3>
</body></html>
```

As you can see, the Nginx service was restarted. At the top of the inserted text, you can see that the state to verify the service is running (roles/webserver/start.sls == roles_webserver_start) was verified as already running. But, thanks to our watch statement, Nginx was restarted. (You can see it in the state with the sites_first ID.) You can play with this by simply updating the source file (*/srv/salt/file/base/sites/src/first.html*) and rerunning the highstate.

The watch functionality uses a function named `mod_watch` inside the state module. Not all states have such a method defined. If a state does not, then it will fall back to using a `require`. You should verify that any state where you use a `watch` directive has a `mod_watch` method declared.

Odds and Ends

This book touches on just a few of the different parts of requisite states. There are just a couple more you should be aware of: `order` and `failhard`. When we looked at the detailed state of a highstate, we saw there was an `order` attribute in the data structure. Salt uses this internally for bookkeeping of the states. Specifically, Salt uses `order` to track the order of each state as it is parsed from the SLS files. There are a couple of options for `order` that may be beneficial.

First, if you want to enforce that a certain state runs first, you can add the `order: 1` declaration to your state. Salt will see this and put that state at the top of the list:

```
[vagrant@master ~]$ cat /srv/salt/file/base/run_first.sls
run_first:
  cmd.run:
  - name: 'echo "I am run first."'
  - order: 1

[vagrant@master ~]$ cat /srv/salt/file/base/top.sls
<snip>
  'minion4.example':
  - users.all
  - run_first

[vagrant@master ~]$ sudo salt minion4.example state.highstate
minion4.example:
  ---------
          ID: run_first
    Function: cmd.run
        Name: echo "I am run first."
      Result: True
     Comment: Command "echo "I am run first."" run
     Started: 23:47:18.232285
    Duration: 10.165 ms
     Changes:
              ----------
              pid:
                  15305
              retcode:
                  0
              stderr:

              stdout:
                  I am run first.
```

```
    - - - - - - - - -
<snip>
Summary
    - - - - - - - - - -
Succeeded: 6 (changed=1)
Failed:    0
    - - - - - - - - - -
Total states run:     6
```

Try removing the order line and then see what the order is. Related to this is the declaration of order: last. As the name suggests, it will make sure that the given state is run last.

Note that using the various requisite states is preferred over using the order command.

The last tidbit is the failhard option. You can add failhard: True to any state. If that state fails to run for any reason, then the entire state (which includes a highstate) will immediately stop. This can prove very useful if you have a service that is absolutely required for your infrastructure to work. If there is any problem deploying this service, stop immediately. You can also add failhard as a global option in the minion configuration.

 cmd.run is very powerful, and it is tempting to use it often. However, there is a caveat here. As you can see, the various requisite states can add a lot of power in ordering your states the way you need. But they need to be able to see any *changes* in states. Also, the test=true command-line argument can help you determine exactly what will happen when a state is run. But cmd.run will always report a change because it *will* run a command. It cannot peer into that command to determine if a particular shell script actually makes any changes or not. As a result, you should use cmd.run in your states only as a last resort.

Docker and Salt

Docker has gained a lot interest since its initial release in 2013. It combines several aspects of the Linux operating system to create a portable *container* that provides resource isolation. This layer of abstraction makes it easier to deploy the same application in multiple environments: development, staging, and production. However, there is a small cost. While not as heavyweight as a complete operating system deployed via a virtual machine, there is a process that manages the deployed containers. This is another process that needs to be managed and monitored.

Salt works with Docker through the docker-ng execution module and the dockerio state module. The details of these modules are beyond the scope of this book.

However, given the high level of interest in Docker containers, we felt it necessary to mention it and encourage you to read up on the ever-evolving state of these modules.[2]

Summary

States are a way for you to define how you want a host, or a set of hosts, to look. You define individual states, like adding a user or installing a package, and then tie them all together using the top file. The top file uses the exact same targeting mechanisms we saw in Chapter 2. You can also define the order in which states run using various requisite states, such as `require` and `watch`. But this is only the beginning of what states can do. We will gain significantly more power when we add the templating engine Jinja in Chapter 6. In the same chapter you will learn how to write your own states.

---

2 The `dockerio` execution module is currently being deprecated.

CHAPTER 5

Minion Data/Master Data

Salt runs on top of other systems—for example, the operating system. But even the operating system runs on top of the hardware. These systems contain a great deal of information that Salt can leverage. Salt's name comes from the fact that there are little bits of information like grains of salt.

Grains Are Minion Data

Grains are calculated when the minion starts. Therefore, they are considered static pieces of data. This is great for information like the version of the operating system or the number of cores in the CPU. This data doesn't change often, and when it does, it likely requires a restart of one of the underlying systems, thus a restart of the minion as well.

This data is all generated on the minion itself. It is then presented to the master for various targeting operations. The Salt minion will have a number of grains set up by default. You can add to them by including a static list or by writing some Python code.

Performing Basic Grain Operations

Let's look at some of the default grains already configured. We can simply list all of these grains on a minion with `grains.ls`:

```
[vagrant@master ~]$ sudo salt master.example grains.ls
master.example:
    - SSDs
    - cpu_flags
    - cpu_model
    - cpuarch
    - domain
```

- fqdn
- fqdn_ip4
- fqdn_ip6
- gpus
- host
- hwaddr_interfaces
- id
- ip4_interfaces
- ip6_interfaces
- ip_interfaces
- ipv4
- ipv6
- kernel
- kernelrelease
- locale_info
- localhost
- lsb_distrib_codename
- lsb_distrib_id
- lsb_distrib_release
- master
- mem_total
- nodename
- num_cpus
- num_gpus
- os
- os_family
- osarch
- oscodename
- osfinger
- osfullname
- osmajorrelease
- osrelease
- osrelease_info
- path
- ps
- pythonexecutable
- pythonpath
- pythonversion
- saltpath
- saltversion
- saltversioninfo
- selinux
- server_id
- shell
- virtual
- zmqversion

As you can see, there is a lot of data available via grains. The preceding example is just
the list of keys. We can use `grains.items` to list all of the keys and their values. Let's
just look at a single value for a moment. A call to `grains.item` os will show the value

of the os grain. To simplify the output a little, we will also introduce an option to the salt command: `--out=txt`:

```
[vagrant@master ~]$ sudo salt \* grains.item os --out=txt
minion2.example: {'os': 'CentOS'}
minion3.example: {'os': 'Ubuntu'}
minion4.example: {'os': 'Ubuntu'}
minion1.example: {'os': 'CentOS'}
master.example: {'os': 'CentOS'}
```

We have been using this command for a while now, especially in Chapter 4 in our top file. Now we want to focus on grains, including setting some of our own.

Setting Grains

We have been using the minion IDs directly to configure them. But this is a little cumbersome. If we had to add a host explicitly every time we created or changed one, it would be extremely tedious. We can use grains to set our own metadata about a host. And then we can target our hosts based on combinations of that data.

Back in Chapter 3, we created a table that listed our minions and some metadata about them. For convenience, we've reproduced that here in Table 5-1.

Table 5-1. Minion IDs, types, and roles

Minion ID	Type	Role
minion1.example	Production (prod)	Web server
		Application server
minion2.example	Production (prod)	Database server
minion3.example	Staging (stage)	Web server
		Application server
		Database server
minion4.example	Development (dev)	Web server
		Application server
		Database server

Let's use this table to set some grains on each minion.

There are several ways to set grains. Right now, we are going to simply set the grains from the Salt master itself. We will set two grains: `myenv` and `roles`:

```
[vagrant@master ~]$ sudo salt -E 'minion(1|2).*' grains.setval myenv prod
minion2.example:
    ----------
    myenv:
        prod
minion1.example:
    ----------
    myenv:
        prod
[vagrant@master ~]$ sudo salt 'minion3.*' grains.setval myenv stage
minion3.example:
    ----------
    myenv:
        stage
[vagrant@master ~]$ sudo salt 'minion4.*' grains.setval myenv dev
minion4.example:
    ----------
    myenv:
        dev

[vagrant@master ~]$ sudo salt 'minion1.*' grains.setval roles \
'[webserver,appserver]'
minion1.example:
    ----------
    roles:
        - webserver
        - appserver
[vagrant@master ~]$ sudo salt 'minion2.*' grains.setval roles \
'[database]'
minion2.example:
    ----------
    roles:
        - database
[vagrant@master ~]$ sudo salt -E 'minion(3|4).*' grains.setval roles \
'[webserver ,appserver,database]'
minion3.example:
    ----------
    roles:
        - webserver
        - appserver
        - database
minion4.example:
    ----------
    roles:
        - webserver
        - appserver
        - database
```

You will notice we made use of a Perl compatible regular expression (PCRE) (*http://www.pcre.org/*) match using the -E flag.

Now, we can query all of these roles with grains.item:

```
[vagrant@master ~]$ sudo salt \* grains.item myenv roles
minion2.example:
    ----------
    myenv:
        prod
    roles:
        - database
minion4.example:
    ----------
    myenv:
        dev
    roles:
        - webserver
        - appserver
        - database
minion3.example:
    ----------
    myenv:
        stage
    roles:
        - webserver
        - appserver
        - database
minion1.example:
    ----------
    myenv:
        prod
    roles:
        - webserver
        - appserver
master.example:
    ----------
```

This data is written into a file, */etc/salt/grains*, so that Salt will retain this data across restarts and even reboots of the operating system. Like so much of Salt, this is a simple YAML file:

```
[vagrant@minion1 ~]$ cat /etc/salt/grains
myenv: prod
roles:
- webserver
- appserver
```

You can also set values in the minion's configuration file, */etc/salt/minion*, by adding it to the grains: declaration.

Targeting with Grains in the Top File

When we first explored the top file, we used grains for the operating system dependencies, but we listed each minion individually for things like users. We can now rewrite the top file using grains:

```
[vagrant@master ~]$ cat /srv/salt/file/base/top.sls
base:
  'os:CentOS':
  - match: grain
  - default.vim-enhanced

  'os:Ubuntu':
  - match: grain
  - default.vim

  'roles:webserver':
  - match: grain
  - roles.webserver
  - sites

  'roles:database':
  - match: grain
  - users.dba

  'myenv:stage':
  - match: grain
  - users.qa

  'myenv:dev':
  - match: grain
  - users.all
  - run_first
```

We have removed all of the targets with minion IDs and replaced them with the relevant grains. We can verify this using state.show_top:

```
[vagrant@master ~]$ sudo salt minion4\* state.show_top
minion4.example:
    ----------
    base:
        - default.vim
        - roles.webserver
        - sites
        - users.dba
        - users.all
        - run_first
```

There are a few changes. For example, all of the states that were targeted only to
minion1 are now targeted to all minions with the grain roles set to the value web
server. You can see how this is much easier to manage than having to add every minion individually.

Grains are a very powerful way of assigning metadata to hosts. But they are mostly
static. Next, we will introduce *pillar* data, which is meant to be more dynamic.

Pillars Are Data from the Master

The first part of this chapter talked about grains—data that is set on the minion. As you've learned, grains are extremely powerful and can be matched in state files or via the Salt command line. The biggest drawback is that they are meant to be relatively static data. What happens if you have data that changes? *Pillars* can solve that problem. Pillar data is stored on the master. But the data is available only for the given minion. So you can have the same key but with different values for different minions. A given minion can only see its own pillar data; it cannot see any pillar data for other minions. Since the channel between the master and the minion is encrypted, pillar data can be thought of as secure to a minion. (Remember that this data is only as secure as your Salt master.)

Querying Pillar Data

Querying pillar data is almost exactly the same as querying grains:

```
[vagrant@master ~]$ sudo salt minion4.example pillar.items
minion4.example:
    ----------
    master:
        ----------
        __pillar:
            True
        __role:
            master
<snip>
        id:
            minion4.example
<snip>
```

There is a lot more, but it is all under a key called `master`. These are actually the master's configuration settings. However, you will notice the `id` set is specific to this minion.

> The output of `pillar.items` can be a little large with the master's configuration data. This can be disabled with the `pillar_opts` configuration value in the master's configuration. Set this to `False`, and the output of `pillar.items` should be a little more manageable. But there is a lot of data in there that can be very useful.

Let's start adding our own data to the pillar. We have been adding the users based on what role each minion played. Initially, we set this explicitly for each minion and then you saw how to use grains to be more efficient. Now, we will use pillar data to set the list of users for each host. Like most of Salt's data, simple pillar data can be stored in a basic YAML file. First, let's set the pillar root in the master's configuration:

```
[vagrant@master ~]$ cat /etc/salt/master.d/pillar.conf
pillar_roots:
  base:
  - /srv/salt/pillar/base
```

You will need to restart the salt-master daemon process to pick up that change.

The setup of pillar data is very similar to that of the state files. The pillar file also needs a top file; it contains targeting information just as with the top file for states:

```
[vagrant@master ~]$ cat /srv/salt/pillar/base/top.sls
base:
  '*':
  - default
```

Next, we'll create a very simple default with some test data, just to get our feet wet:

```
[vagrant@master ~]$ cat /srv/salt/pillar/base/default.sls
my_data: some data for stuff
```

We can create some user data for each group of users. Let's create a pillar that contains all users, one for just the staging users, and then a specific one for the DBA:

```
[vagrant@master ~]$ cat /srv/salt/pillar/base/users/all.sls
users:
  wilma: 2001
  fred: 2002
  barney: 2003
  betty: 2004
[vagrant@master ~]$ cat /srv/salt/pillar/base/users/stage.sls
users:
  wilma: 2001
  barney: 2003
  betty: 2004
[vagrant@master ~]$ cat /srv/salt/pillar/base/users/dba.sls
users:
  wilma: 2001
```

So far this looks very similar to the states we saw in the previous chapter. However, there is a big difference: you cannot *call* a pillar file individually like we did with *state.sls*. Rather, the entire collection of files is compiled together to create one large data set available to the minion. So we need a *top.sls* file to pull it all together:

```
[vagrant@master ~]$ cat /srv/salt/pillar/base/top.sls
base:
  '*':
  - default

  'G@myenv:prod and G@roles:database':
  - match: compound
  - users.dba

  'myenv:stage':
  - match: grain
```

```
    - users.stage

  'myenv:dev':
  - match: grain
  - users.all
```

We can now query the user pillar data for every minion:

```
[vagrant@master ~]$ sudo salt \* pillar.item users
minion3.example:
    ----------
    users:
        ----------
        barney:
            2003
        betty:
            2004
        wilma:
            2001
minion4.example:
    ----------
    users:
        ----------
        barney:
            2003
        betty:
            2004
        fred:
            2002
        wilma:
            2001
minion2.example:
    ----------
    users:
        ----------
        wilma:
            2001
minion1.example:
    ----------
master.example:
    ----------
```

This is all great, but it seems to duplicate the data we already have in the state files. This discussion is just meant to introduce pillar data.

> In"Introduction to Jinja" on page 83, we introduce the templating language Jinja, which will allow us to pull all of this together.

Querying Other Sources with External Pillars

The pillar system provides a data layer, but the data must all be in YAML files within the pillar file tree. Often, you will have data in other data sources. You can query these other systems using external pillars (ext_pillar). The *external pillar* system has several built-in options for querying these other systems. The built-ins range from MySQL to Git to Amazon's S3. In order to keep things simple, we are going to look at the cmd_yaml module.

The cmd_yaml external pillar simply runs a command and then parses the output as YAML and adds it to the pillar data. As with all pillars, external pillars are run on the master, not the minions. As a result, the command only needs to be available on your master. Also, since it just needs to be available to the Salt master somewhere on the filesystem, it does not need to be anywhere within the file layout we have discussed. (For example, it does not have to be in the *file_roots* or *pillar_roots* directory.) We will create a very simple bash script to return the list of users:

```
[vagrant@master ~]$ cat /srv/salt/scripts/user-pillar.sh
#!/bin/bash
echo "users:"
echo " app: 9001"
```

Earlier, we said that the data that comes from the external pillar is *added* to the pillar data. Salt will merge data from the external pillar into the existing pillar data. Since we already have our users defined, let's just add another user we want on all hosts: app.

Let's look at the users for the minion that has all users defined: minion4:

```
[vagrant@master ~]$ sudo salt minion4.example pillar.item users
minion4.example:
    ----------
    users:
        ----------
        app:
            9001
        barney:
            2003
        betty:
            2004
        fred:
            2002
        wilma:
            2001
```

As we've said, using pillar data does not appear to be very useful at the moment. We have merely duplicated data in the state files and in the pillar files. However, we will remedy this in Chapter 6 with the default templating engine, Jinja. But before heading there, we should briefly mention a few data options other than YAML and Jinja.

Renderers Give Data Options

Until now, we have focused on the default file formats. Specifically, all of the files we have edited have been in YAML. Since Salt is all written in Python, everything will eventually be translated into Python data structures. As long as the core Salt code receives data in a format it understands, it doesn't matter how that data is edited or what format any files are in. The core Salt code will translate formats using *renderers*.

Rendering directly from YAML is simple enough. However, the default case also includes support for the powerful templating engine Jinja. When Salt needs data, either from a state file (SLS) or from a pillar, the file is first parsed using the templating engine. At that point, the file should be in a data format that Salt understands. (Again, in the default case the data is in YAML.) It is important to understand these two phases since you can change either of them.

As of version 2014.1, Salt ships with support for the combinations shown in Table 5-2.

Table 5-2. Templating engines and data formats currently supported in Salt

Templating engine	Data format
Jinja	YAML
Mako	YAML
Wempy	YAML
Jinja	JSON
Mako	JSON
Wempy	JSON

The default renderer is specified in the master config with the `renderer` config option.

 If you have not edited the default configuation that ships with Salt, you should see the default case commented out:

```
#renderer: yaml_jinja
```

The different combinations of data formats and templating engines give you a number of options. This should make it easier to integrate the data sources with third parties or even to write your own code given your company's preferences.

This book focuses only on using YAML with Jinja templates. (As noted, we will give a quick introduction to Jinja in the next chapter.) But just to give you a feel for the power it offers, we will compose a very simple example using JSON.

We don't want to change how any of our current files are read. So we are not going to change the master's configuration option (renderer). Rather, we can change the renderer on a file-by-file basis using the *shebang* syntax (#!) common to Unix scripts:

```
[vagrant@master ~]$ cat /srv/salt/file/base/json.sls
#!json
{
  "json_test": {
    "cmd.run": [
      {
        "name": "echo \"Json test\""
      }
    ]
  }
}
```

The first line contains the shebang type directive. (Notice that it is not a full path, just the renderer to use.) The rest of the file is standard JSON we've laid out with dictionaries and lists just as we did with YAML. Let's look at how Salt will interpret this file:

```
[vagrant@master ~]$ sudo salt master\* state.show_sls json
master.example:
    ----------
    json_test:
        ----------
        __env__:
            base
        __sls__:
            json
        cmd:
            |_
              ----------
              name:
                  echo "Json test"
            - run
            |_
              ----------
              order:
                  10000
```

This is exactly the same as our other files. This example further illustrates that all of these files are just data to Salt. YAML is simply the default format.

Now, let's run this state to verify that it all works as expected:

```
[vagrant@master ~]$ sudo salt master\* state.sls json
master.example:
 ---------
          ID: json_test
    Function: cmd.run
        Name: echo "Json test"
      Result: True
     Comment: Command "echo "Json test"" run
     Started: 17:34:03.534634
    Duration: 7.617 ms
     Changes:
              ----------
              pid:
                  4262
              retcode:
                  0
              stderr:

              stdout:
                  Json test

Summary
 ----------
Succeeded: 1 (changed=1)
Failed:    0
 ----------
Total states run:      1
```

While there are several options that ship with Salt, including the ability to add any renderer you prefer, we are going to use YAML (and, soon, Jinja templates) throughout this book. But as long as Salt can get the data into its own data structure, you have plenty of options for how you store that data.

CHAPTER 6

Extending Salt: Part I

If you were to put this book down right now, you should be able to successfully use Salt to solve a wide variety of problems. A standard install of Salt provides a number of execution modules that can allow you to maintain a number of off-the-shelf components. When combined with states and pillars, these standard tools allow you to accomplish a great deal. However, you will likely need to do something that Salt does not handle by default, whether it's building a custom module to manage some software you wrote at your company, or creating a custom grain that makes available some company-specific piece of data. Each piece we have discussed thus far can be customized. In this chapter, we introduce a few elements to customizing some of the data focused on a specific minion.

Introduction to Jinja

The data files that Salt uses have a very straightforward syntax. In fact, in the default case, they are just YAML files. But in the end, they are just data. They don't allow for any complex logic. This is where Jinja templates can help.

Jinja is a very powerful templating engine best known for its use in the Flask web framework. Jinja is complicated, and is a language in its own right. We only intend to introduce just enough of the Jinja language so you are able to add logic to your data files. A comprehensive tutorial is beyond the scope of this book. However, the Jinja site (*http://jinja.pocoo.org/*) has great documentation.

Jinja Basics

Let's start with a simple example so you can get a feel for Jinja:

```
{% set my_name = 'Barney' %}
Hi {{ my_name }}!
```

This will give the following output:

```
Hi Barney!
```

The first thing you should notice is the use of the curly brace as the delimiter. Also notice how, when we set the variable, we used, {% … %}; on the next line, when we needed to display the variable, we wrote {{ … }}. The first format is used for various control structures (e.g., for loops, if blocks, etc.), while the latter (double brace) syntax makes for a print statement. Lastly, there is {# … #}. This is a simple comment block.

Before we continue, let's discuss how various statements can be tested. Since the plan is to incorporate with Salt, we can use a Salt command. Earlier, we used the state.show_sls function when viewing states. We can use the same function now to show the output of Jinja commands. Let's create a "dummy" state file:

```
[vagrant@master ~]$ cat /srv/salt/file/base/jinja/simple_var.sls
{% set simple_var = 'a simple variable' %}
jinja_var:
  cmd.run:
  - name: echo "Simple var is {{ simple_var }}"
```

Then we can run that and see the output of the Jinja variables:

```
[vagrant@master ~]$ sudo salt master.example state.show_sls jinja.simple_var
master.example:
    ----------
    jinja_var:
        ----------
        __env__:
            base
        __sls__:
            jinja.simple_var
        cmd:
            |_
              ----------
              name:
                  echo "Simple var is a simple variable"
            - run
            |_
              ----------
              order:
                  10000
```

 The output of show_sls for the purpose of demonstrating Jinja templates is a little too verbose. We will be parsing the output to show only the most relevant material. Just keep in mind that when you run the command as shown, you should see quite a bit more output.

As you can see, the substitution for `simple_var` happens when the state is compiled, not when it is run.

Jinja has a lot more than just strings. It also has lists (arrays):

```
[vagrant@master ~]$ cat /srv/salt/file/base/jinja/list.sls
{% set list1 = ['one', 'two', 'three'] %}
jinja_list:
  cmd.run:
  - name: echo "List is {{ list1 }}"

[vagrant@master ~]$ sudo salt master.example state.show_sls jinja.list
master.example:
    ----------
    jinja_list:
<snip>
            name:
                echo "List is ['one', 'two', 'three']"
    <snip>
```

You can view a single item from a list just as you do in Python:

```
[vagrant@master ~]$ cat /srv/salt/file/base/jinja/list_item.sls
{% set list1 = ['one', 'two', 'three'] %}
jinja_list_item:
  cmd.run:
  - name: echo "List item 2 is {{ list1[2] }}"

[vagrant@master ~]$ sudo salt master.example state.show_sls jinja.list_item
master.example:
    ----------
    jinja_list_item:
<snip>
            name:
                echo "List item 2 is three"
    <snip>
```

Jinja includes dictionaries (hashes) as well. And, just as with the list type, you can refer to an individual item using the same syntax as you would use in Python:

```
[vagrant@master ~]$ cat /srv/salt/file/base/jinja/dict.sls
{% set my_dict = {'first': 'value 1', 'second': 'value 2'} %}
jinja_dict_first:
  cmd.run:
  - name: echo "First item is {{ my_dict['first'] }}"

[vagrant@master ~]$ sudo salt master.example state.show_sls jinja.dict
master.example:
    ----------
    jinja_dict_first:
<snip>
            name:
                echo "First item is value 1"
    <snip>
```

You will find that a lot of the syntax in Jinja is very similar to Python. A number of Python functions are also supported, for example, listing the keys of a dictionary:

```
[vagrant@master ~]$ cat /srv/salt/file/base/jinja/keys.sls
{% set my_dict = {'first': 'value 1', 'second': 'value 2'} %}
jinja_keys:
  cmd.run:
  - name: echo "Keys are {{ my_dict.keys() }}"

[vagrant@master ~]$ sudo salt master.example state.show_sls jinja.keys
master.example:
    ----------
    jinja_keys:
<snip>
            name:
                echo "Keys are ['second', 'first']"
<snip>
```

Basic control structures

Jinja has a number of standard control structures, for example, if statements and for loops. Since they are control structures, they need to be encapsulated within the {% ... %} syntax. Until now, Jinja statements should look very familiar to a Python programmer. Lists and dictionaries have a similar look and feel. Even some of the methods of both are exposed. But with control structures, things start to differ.

You have to remember that Jinja is a general-purpose templating language. It is used to generate HTML pages, among other things. As a result, the "indentation" method of delimiting blocks of text does not work. So control structures need to explicitly mark the end of the block.

Let's look at a simple example of an if statement:

```
[vagrant@master ~]$ cat /srv/salt/file/base/jinja/if.sls
{% set my_bool = true %}
jinja_if:
  cmd.run:
  {% if my_bool %}
  - name: 'echo "It is true."'
  {% else %}
  - name: 'echo "Is it not true."'
  {% endif %}

[vagrant@master ~]$ sudo salt master.example state.show_sls jinja.if
master.example:
    ----------
    jinja_if:
<snip>
            name:
                echo "It is true."
<snip>
```

The basic keywords should look very familiar: `if`, `else`, and `endif`.

 Remember that the renderer will pass any files through the Jinja templating engine before parsing them as YAML and then as a Salt data structure. As a result, if Jinja removes any statements, Salt itself will never see them. In the preceding example, if there were a syntax error in the `else` block, the renderer would never see it.

Next is a simple `for` loop. As with the `if` statement, this should look very familiar:

```
[vagrant@master ~]$ cat /srv/salt/file/base/jinja/for.sls
{% set my_list = ['a', 'b', 'c'] %}
{% for current in my_list %}
jinja_for_{{ current }}:
  cmd.run:
  - name: "echo 'Current value is {{ current }}'"
{% endfor %}

[vagrant@master ~]$ sudo salt master.example state.show_sls jinja.for
master.example:
    ----------
    jinja_for_a:
<snip>
            name:
                echo 'Current value is a'
<snip>
    jinja_for_b:
<snip>
            name:
                echo 'Current value is b'
<snip>
    jinja_for_c:
<snip>
            name:
                echo 'Current value is c'
<snip>
```

Other Jinja statements

There are just a few other Jinja statements that will come in handy: `macro`, `include`, and `import`. The `macro` statement allows several statements to be executed as a single, logical block. You can think of a macro as a mini-template. It allows you to collect many things together and then refer to them using a single Jinja command. You can define a number of input arguments and then execute the necessary code. Here's a very simple example to emphasize this point:

```
[vagrant@master ~]$ cat /srv/salt/file/base/jinja/macro.sls
{% macro exclaim(string) -%}
{{ string + '!!!' -}}
{%- endmacro %}
```

```
jinja_macro:
  cmd.run:
  - name: "echo {{ exclaim('Yay') }}"

[vagrant@master ~]$ sudo salt master.example state.show_sls jinja.macro
master.example:
    ----------
    jinja_macro:
<snip>
            name:
                echo Yay!!!
    <snip>
```

One of the first things you'll notice is that there isn't a return from the macro. It simply prints the output, which is then propagated back to the caller. You should also notice the dashes (-) near the various delimiters. A dash signals Jinja to remove the end-of-line character from the text. Remember that Jinja is a templating engine, so it is designed to add the text as given, including end-of-line characters. Thus far, this hasn't been a problem. But if those end-of-line characters are added to the preceding SLS, then the text following the colon appears on the following line, and that is not valid YAML. Rest assured, this is a bit of an edge case. Just be aware of how Jinja behaves and that the dash can help in situations like the preceding one.

The `include` statement allows you to pull in rendered data from other files:

```
[vagrant@master ~]$ cat /srv/salt/file/base/jinja/include.sls
{% include 'jinja/some_vars.jinja'  with context %}

[vagrant@master ~]$ cat /srv/salt/file/base/jinja/some_vars.jinja
{% set var = 'the string' %}
some_var_include:
  cmd.run:
  - name: "echo 'From include, var is {{ var }}'"

[vagrant@master ~]$ sudo salt master.example state.show_sls jinja.include
master.example:
    ----------
    some_var_include:
<snip>
            name:
                echo 'From include, var is the string'
    <snip>
```

> Remember that files are included via Jinja before Salt can parse the data. Be careful to not duplicate state IDs.

Be careful: files that are pulled in via the `include` statement *are* rendered. So the variables used in the second file *will not* be available to any files that `include` that file. If you would like to use the Jinja variables, use the `import` statement. Again, the format is reminiscent of Python code:

```
[vagrant@master ~]$ cat /srv/salt/file/base/jinja/vars.jinja
{% set my_var = 'more strings' %}

[vagrant@master ~]$ cat /srv/salt/file/base/jinja/from.sls
{% from "jinja/vars.jinja" import my_var as the_var with context %}
jinja_from:
  cmd.run:
  - name: "echo 'The var is {{ the_var }}'"

[vagrant@master ~]$ sudo salt master.example state.show_sls jinja.from
master.example:
    ----------
    jinja_from:
<snip>
            name:
                echo 'The var is more strings'
<snip>
```

Multiple variables can be included as well. Just list them, separated by commas, much like you would in Python.

This discussion only scratches the surface of Jinja's capabilities, but it is sufficient for introducing the power Jinja can bring to your states and pillars. Refer to the Jinja website for more details on its features.[1]

Templating with Jinja

So far, we have just shown the basics of Jinja with very little Salt-specific features. Salt does add a number of additional features on top of Jinja. Salt will expose grains, pillar data, and even execution *modules* within Jinja files.[2]

Let's take a very simple example of using the minion ID:

```
[vagrant@master ~]$ cat /srv/salt/file/base/jinja/grains.sls
{% set name = grains['id'] %}
jinja_grains:
  cmd.run:
  - name: "echo 'My name is {{ name }}'"

[vagrant@master ~]$ sudo salt master.example state.show_sls jinja.grains
master.example:
    ----------
    jinja_grains:
<snip>
```

---

1 Refer to the following page for more information on Salt-specific details regarding Jinja: *http://bit.ly/jinja_salt*.

2 Salt will also expose opts, sls, and env into Jinja templates.

```
      name:
          echo 'My name is master.example'
  <snip>
```

Grains and pillar data are available within Jinja templates as their own dictionaries.

The execution modules are available within a dictionary named `salt`:

```
[vagrant@master ~]$ cat /srv/salt/file/base/jinja/cmd.sls
{% set who = salt['cmd.run']('whoami') %}
jinja_cmd:
  cmd.run:
  - name: "echo 'Whoami gives {{ who }}'"

[vagrant@master ~]$ sudo salt master.example state.show_sls jinja.cmd
master.example:
    ----------
    jinja_cmd:
<snip>
            name:
                echo 'Whoami gives root'
  <snip>
```

You'll notice that the execution module is given as the value in the `salt` dictionary. Following that come any arguments that may be required.

Earlier we discussed importing variables from other Jinja files. This allows you to share variables with a number of different state files or in pillar definitions. If you want to be able to use the Salt-provided dictionaries, however, you need to tell Jinja to import the *context*. At the end of your `import` (or `from`) statement, be sure to add the phrase `with context`. This will alert the parsing libraries to expose all of Salt's data structures to the child, or imported, file.

Filtering by Grains

With all of the execution modules available, you have a significant number of options for creating very sophisticated states and pillars. However, one specific command needs to be called out: `grains.filter_by`. This command allows you to take a data set and parse out the piece needed based on a grain value:

```
[vagrant@master ~]$ cat /srv/salt/file/base/show_users.sls
{% set all_users = {
    'master.example': [],
    'minion1.example': [],
    'minion2.example': ['wilma'],
    'minion3.example': ['wilma', 'barney', 'betty'],
    'minion4.example': ['wilma', 'barney', 'betty', 'fred'],
} %}
{% set cur_users = salt['grains.filter_by'](all_users, grain='id') %}
show_users:
```

```
    cmd.run:
    - name: "echo 'User list is {{ cur_users }}'"

[vagrant@master ~]$ sudo salt minion4\* state.sls show_users
minion4.example:
  ---------
          ID: show_users
<snip>
            stdout:
                User list is [wilma, barney, betty, fred]
<snip>
```

The dictionary all_users lists some values, with key being the minion ID. Remember that the default install of Salt sets up a number of grains for you to use. The grains provide data such as the name of the operating system, the number of CPUs in the host, and even the version of Salt running. When they are combined with the grains.filter_by function, you can build a data set that can be customized to any number of special cases.

Custom Execution Module

We have talked a lot about how Salt can be customized in a bunch of different ways. Jinja provides a powerful templating engine that, when combined with Salt's features, exposes a great deal of functionality. However, it is likely that at some point you will need to automate a task that would be very difficult with Jinja, states, and the host of other powerful Salt features. Fortunately, Salt provides a way for you to simply write some Python code and execute it on every host.

No programming book would be complete without a "Hello, world" example:

```
hello.py
"""
A collection of simple examples.
"""

def world():
    """
    The simplest of examples.

    CLI Example::

        salt '*' hello.world
    """
    return 'Hello, world.'
```

The preceding code includes some simple examples of docstrings. Using docstrings within your custom modules is considered a best practice, and it is highly encouraged. You can simply use sys.doc with your module name to see the output.

The first obvious question is "Where do I put this file?"

Up until now, *file_roots* has contained only state files and maybe a few Jinja files. But there are a couple of "reserved directories": *_modules*, *_grains*, and *_states*. The first one, *_modules*, is where execution modules are kept. (The other two will be discussed shortly.) Create the preceding file, *hello.py*, and place it in */srv/salt/files/base/_modules*. If you try to execute it, you will likely see the following:

```
[vagrant@master ~]$ sudo salt master.example hello.world
master.example:
    'hello.world' is not available.
```

Earlier, we mentioned that the minions may need to *sync* to see, as an example, pillar data. With states, Salt will sync as part of the process of executing the state. However, this is not true with modules. You will need to sync module changes (including the addition of new modules) using the `saltutil` command:

```
[vagrant@master ~]$ sudo salt \* saltutil.sync_modules
minion4.example:
    - modules.hello
minion3.example:
    - modules.hello
minion1.example:
    - modules.hello
minion2.example:
    - modules.hello
master.example:
    - modules.hello
```

This will return any changed modules that were loaded onto the respective minion. Since each minion received our new module, let's run it:

```
[vagrant@master ~]$ sudo salt \* hello.world
minion2.example:
    Hello, world.
minion1.example:
    Hello, world.
minion4.example:
    Hello, world.
minion3.example:
    Hello, world.
master.example:
    Hello, world.
```

The function `saltutil.sync_modules` will copy the modules from the master to the cache directory on each minion. Once the files are copied over, the *loader* will need to find the public functions. To do this, it runs parts of the code at this point. For example, any code not in a method will be run during this load. Be careful about the code you do not put into methods. Also, this means there is a delay between when the sync completes and when you are actually able to run the new module. This delay is usually just a minute or two.

As with Jinja templates, Salt adds some custom data into the module's namespace: `grains` ,`salt`, and `opts`. They are all dictionaries, and as with Jinja, the `salt` dictionary exposes the entire wealth of execution modules. The `opts` dictionary gives you access to various minion configuration settings. Let's add a simple call to the `grains` dictionary:

```
[vagrant@master ~]$ cat /srv/salt/file/base/_modules/hello.py
"""
A collection of simple examples.
"""
def world():
    """
    The simplest of examples.

    CLI Example::

        salt '*' hello.world
    """
    return 'Hello, world.'

def id():
    """
    Better example using the minion id.

    CLI Example::

        salt '*' hello.id
    """
    id = __grains__['id']
    return 'Hello, {0}.'.format(id)
[vagrant@master ~]$ sudo salt \* hello.id
minion3.example:
    Hello, minion3.example.
minion4.example:
    Hello, minion4.example.
minion2.example:
    Hello, minion2.example.
minion1.example:
    Hello, minion1.example.
```

```
master.example:
    Hello, master.example.
```

(Don't forget to sync the modules with salt * saltutil.sync_modules and give it a minute to load the code.)

Let's see what the documentation looks like:

```
[vagrant@master ~]$ sudo salt-call sys.doc hello
local:
    ----------
    hello.id:

            Better example using the minion id.

            CLI Example::

                salt '*' hello.id

    hello.world:

            The simplest of examples.

            CLI Example::

                salt '*' hello.world
```

There's one last bit of housekeeping to do: logging. It is good form to import the logging module and give some feedback as to how your new module is running:

```
[vagrant@master ~]$ cat /srv/salt/file/base/_modules/hello.py
"""
A collection of simple examples.
"""
import logging
logger = logging.getLogger(__name__)

def world():
    """
    The simplest of examples.

    CLI Example::

        salt '*' hello.world
    """
    return 'Hello, world.'

def id():
    """
    Better example using the minion id.

    CLI Example::
```

```
    salt '*' hello.id
    """
id = __grains__['id']
logger.debug('Found grain id: {0}'.format(id))
return 'Hello, {0}.'.format(id)
```

 The preceding example does not conform to PEP 8 (Python Enhancement Proposals) standards. We are minimizing the amount of blank lines to help keep the output concise for the book, but please use the proper PEP standards when coding.

In order to see the output from the logger, you need to use `salt-call`. When the module executes on each minion, only the return data is sent back to the master. Any logging output will be sent to the minion's logs (depending on your configuration). But you can run `salt-call` with `log-level` set to `debug` to see the full output. (Remember, the minion runs the code, so you will need to sync your modules again before running `salt-call`.)

```
[vagrant@master ~]$ sudo salt-call --log-level=debug hello.id
<snip>
[DEBUG   ] Found grain id: master.example
[DEBUG   ] LazyLoaded .returner
[DEBUG   ] Decrypting the current master AES key
[DEBUG   ] Loaded minion key: /etc/salt/pki/minion/minion.pem
local:
    Hello, master.example.
```

Custom State Modules

Custom execution modules give you a great deal of power and have a very easy-to-understand format. However, integrating with the state system exposes a lot more possibilities. The format of a custom state module has a few more rules you should follow.

As we previously mentioned, there is a reserved subdirectory inside the file root called _states_. The first big difference with custom states, as opposed to execution modules, is that custom state modules should respect the `test=True` argument. Next, the format of the returned data structure has to be a dictionary with the following keys: `name`, `changes`, `result`, and `comment`. The `name` and `comment` fields should be pretty self-explanatory. The `changes` key has as its value a dictionary with the changes listed. Lastly, `result` just gives a Boolean value (`True` or `False`) so that Salt knows whether the state succeeded or not:

```
[vagrant@master ~]$ more /srv/salt/file/base/_states/custom.py
import os

def enforce_tmp(name, contents=None):
    """
    Enforce a temp file has the desired contents.

    name
        The name of the file to change. (Under '/tmp'.)
    contents
        The value you will be storing.
    """

    return_dict = {
        'name': name,
        'changes': {},
        'result': False,
        'comment': ''
    }

    tmp_file = os.path.join('/tmp', name)
    file_ok = False
    content_ok = False
    file_contents = None

    if os.path.isfile(tmp_file):
        file_ok = True
        with open(tmp_file, 'r') as fp:
            file_contents = fp.read()
            file_contents = file_contents.rstrip('\n')

    if file_contents == contents:
        content_ok = True

    comments = ""
    if file_ok:
        comments += 'File exists ({0})\n'.format(tmp_file)
    else:
        comments += 'File created ({0})\n'.format(tmp_file)
    if content_ok:
        comments += 'Contents correct ({0})\n'.format(file_contents)
    else:
        comments += 'Contents updated ({0})\n'.format(contents)
    return_dict['comment'] = comments

    # Check if this is a test run, if so do not change anything.
    if __opts__['test'] == True:
        return_dict['result'] = None
        return_dict['changes'] = {}
        if not content_ok:
            return_dict['comment'] = {
                'contents': {
```

```
                    'old': file_contents,
                    'new': contents
                }
            }
        return return_dict

    if not content_ok:
        with open(tmp_file, 'w') as fp:
            contents += "\n"
            fp.write(contents)
        return_dict['result'] = True
        return_dict['changes'] = {
            'contents': {
                'old': file_contents,
                'new': contents
            }
        }
    else:
        return_dict['changes'] = {}
        return_dict['result'] = True

    return return_dict
```

Then the accompanying state file:

```
[vagrant@master ~]$ cat /srv/salt/file/base/custom.sls
custom_state:
  custom.enforce_tmp:
  - name: foo
  - contents: bar
```

The custom.enforce_tmp takes as its arguments the name of a file (which will live in /tmp) and then the desired contents of that file.

We want to make sure there is no file named /tmp/foo, after which we can run our new state (custom) that uses our new state execution function:

```
[vagrant@master ~]$ ls /tmp/foo
ls: cannot access /tmp/foo: No such file or directory
[vagrant@master ~]$ sudo salt master.example state.sls custom
master.example:
  ----------
            ID: custom_state
      Function: custom.enforce_tmp
          Name: foo
        Result: True
       Comment: File created (/tmp/foo)
                Contents updated (bar)
       Started: 07:10:41.950351
      Duration: 0.532 ms
       Changes:
                ----------
                contents:
```

```
                 ----------
         new:
                 bar

         old:
                 None

Summary
----------
Succeeded: 1 (changed=1)
Failed:    0
----------
Total states run:      1

[vagrant@master ~]$ cat /tmp/foo
bar
```

While the custom execution module was far easier to write, hopefully you can see the power you gain by writing a custom state module and then using it in your states. We could have easily written our simple example using an execution module, but then we wouldn't have had the additional power that comes with the test=true flag:

```
[vagrant@master ~]$ sudo salt master.example state.sls custom test=true
master.example:
    ---------
            ID: custom_state
      Function: custom.enforce_tmp
          Name: foo
        Result: None
       Comment: File exists (/tmp/foo)
                Contents correct (bar)
       Started: 07:13:50.174386
      Duration: 0.63 ms
       Changes:

Summary
----------
Succeeded: 1 (unchanged=1)
Failed:    0
----------
Total states run:      1
```

Custom Grains

As you have seen, grains provide a powerful method to annotate hosts. But up until now, you had to manually set these grains on every host. However, with custom grains, you can have your minions automatically set their grains.

It's important to remember that grains are meant to contain relatively static information. You can set grains using the `grains.setval` function. For data that changes often, or that is very specific to a small number of hosts, you may want to consider using pillar data instead.

As with custom modules, there is a specific directory for grains modules. All of your custom grains need to go into the _grains_ subdirectory within the *file_roots* directory. (In this specific case, this means that all grains should be in the directory */srv/salt/ files/base/_grains*.)

Earlier, we set the grains for our hosts manually using the `grains.setval` function. We are going to move that to a custom grains module. This example is very brute-force; each minion is listed with the grains we want to set. But you can easily extrapolate this concept to query some kind of *metadata store* that lists all of the various pieces of metadata related to your hosts:

```
[vagrant@master ~]$ cat /srv/salt/file/base/_grains/my_grains.py
"""
Custom grains for the example hosts.
"""
import platform
import logging
logger = logging.getLogger(__name__)

def _get_hostname():
    hostname = platform.node()
    logger.debug('Using hostname: {0}'.format(hostname))
    return hostname

def set_myenv():
    """
    Set the 'myenv' grain based on the host name.
    """
    grains = {}
    hostname = _get_hostname()
    if hostname.startswith('minion1'):
        grains['myenv'] = 'prod'
    elif hostname.startswith('minion2'):
        grains['myenv'] = 'prod'
    elif hostname.startswith('minion3'):
        grains['myenv'] = 'stage'
    elif hostname.startswith('minion4'):
        grains['myenv'] = 'dev'
    return grains

def set_roles():
    """
    Set the 'roles" grain based on the host name.
    """
```

```
grains = {}
hostname = _get_hostname()
if hostname.startswith('minion1'):
    grains['roles'] = ['webserver', 'appserver']
elif hostname.startswith('minion2'):
    grains['roles'] = ['database']
elif hostname.startswith('minion3'):
    grains['roles'] = ['webserver', 'appserver', 'database']
elif hostname.startswith('minion4'):
    grains['roles'] = ['webserver', 'appserver', 'database']
return grains
```

Without a custom execution module, the naming was very simple. If the method were *public* (i.e., the name did not have a leading underscore, _), then that method (or function) would be available to be called via the salt command. Also, with custom state modules, you have to call the function by module name and function. Custom grains work a little bit differently. When a custom grain module is loaded, all of the public functions are executed and all of their return data (dictionaries) is merged into the complete set of grains. As a result, we have written our custom grain with three different functions. The first, _get_hostname(), is considered *private* and is not directly called via the grains loader, but is available for use elsewhere in that module. The next two, set_myenv() and set_roles(), are both called whenever the custom grains module is loaded. There is nothing special about the method names; Salt will simply run every nonprivate function.

The first thing we need to do is to remove our custom grains:

```
[vagrant@master ~]$ sudo salt \* cmd.run 'rm /etc/salt/grains'
minion1.example:

minion4.example:

minion2.example:

minion3.example:

master.example:
    rm: cannot remove `/etc/salt/grains': No such file or directory
```

 If you remember, we did not set any grains on the master. So it should not be a surprise that the *grains* file was not found.

Next, we should restart the minions to be extra sure there are no remnants of the old grains lying around:

```
[vagrant@master ~]$ sudo salt \* service.restart salt-minion
```

Don't forget that you must sync the grains in order to get your new grains module out to all of the minions. You can sync directly using `saltutil.sync_grains` or `saltutil.sync_all`. Also, grains modules will be synced automatically whenever `state.highstate` is run:

```
[vagrant@master ~]$ sudo salt \* saltutil.sync_grains
```

Then we can call `grains.item` to make sure all of our custom grains are available again:

```
[vagrant@master ~]$ sudo salt \* grains.item myenv roles
minion2.example:
    ----------
    myenv:
        prod
    roles:
        - database
minion3.example:
    ----------
    myenv:
        stage
    roles:
        - webserver
        - appserver
        - database
minion1.example:
    ----------
    myenv:
        prod
    roles:
        - webserver
        - appserver
minion4.example:
    ----------
    myenv:
        dev
    roles:
        - webserver
        - appserver
        - database
master.example:
    ----------
```

We have talked about a couple of different ways to set grains on hosts. Before we continue, we should quickly mention the order of precedence for how grains are set:

1. Core grains (from Salt itself)
2. Custom grain modules
3. Custom grains in */etc/salt/grains*

4. Custom grains in the minion configuration

Therefore, if you want to ensure that a grain will not be overwritten, you will want to put it directly into your minion configuration. (You could create a specific file to make it easier to manage: *etc/salt/minion.d/grains.conf*.)

It's important to remember that this code will be executed every time the grains are calculated. Be careful not to execute code that will consume a great deal of system resources or take too long to complete.

External Pillars

Back in Chapter 5, we saw how we could grab pillar data that was outside the `pillar_roots` by using an external pillar (`ext_pillar`). While Salt comes with several `ext_pillar` modules, there are always cases where your data is not in a system where it is easy to export the data into YAML or JSON. Writing a custom external pillar module gives you the flexibility to retrieve data from any source as long as you can write some Python to get at it.

If you recall, one of the chief aspects of pillar data is that it is run on the master, but the data is specific to every minion. In our earlier example with `cmd_yaml`, there wasn't any option to target the data by minion, so every minion got the same list of users. This is a limitation in the `cmd_yaml` module, specifically. Let's expand on that basic concept so we can set the users per host.

 Just as a point of fact, the `cmd_yaml` module is *meant* to be an example. So it is not surprising that it uses only the most basic of functionality. Like most of the examples in this book, it is intended as a framework from which you can build your own solutions.

The first thing we need to do is set the `extension_modules` configuration option in the master's config:

```
[vagrant@master ~]$ cat /etc/salt/master.d/ext-modules.conf
extension_modules: /srv/salt/modules
```

(Don't forget to restart the `salt-master` service.)

Next, let's add our new external pillar:

```
[vagrant@master ~]$ more /srv/salt/modules/pillar/my_users.py

def __virtual__():
    return True


__all_users = {
    'wilma': {'uid': 2001, 'full': 'Wilma Flintstone'},
```

```
        'fred': {'uid': 2002, 'full': 'Fred Flintstone'},
        'barney': {'uid': 2003, 'full': 'Barney Rubble'},
        'betty': {'uid': 2004, 'full': 'Betty Rubble'},
        'app': {'uid': 9001, 'full': 'App User'},
    }

def ext_pillar(minion_id, pillar, *args, **kwargs):
    """
    Return the list of users for the given minion.
    """
    users = {}
    users['app'] = __all_users['app']
    if minion_id == 'minion1.example':
        pass
    elif minion_id == 'minion2.example':
        users['wilma'] = __all_users['wilma']
    elif minion_id == 'minion3.example':
        users['wilma'] = __all_users['wilma']
        users['barney'] = __all_users['barney']
        users['betty'] = __all_users['betty']
    elif minion_id == 'minion4.example':
        users['wilma'] = __all_users['wilma']
        users['barney'] = __all_users['barney']
        users['betty'] = __all_users['betty']
        users['fred'] = __all_users['fred']
    return {'my_users': users}
```

Again, this is *very* brute-force. We are not trying to be overly cute; we are explicitly listing the users for each minion ID. The goal is to show how you can dynamically generate your data and feed it into the pillar system. Once you have the basic concept, you can expand it to call whatever *source of truth* you use to manage your users.

Please note that we are returning the user list into my_users. Back in Chapter 4, we were storing the user data in a pillar simply named users. Using a different key name will make it easier to demonstrate how we are migrating from the old way to the new way.

Next, we need to add our new, custom, external pillar to our list of external pillars:

```
[vagrant@master ~]$ more /etc/salt/master.d/pillar.conf
pillar_roots:
  base:
   - /srv/salt/pillar/base

ext_pillar:
  - my_users: []
#  - cmd_yaml: bash /srv/salt/scripts/user-pillar.sh
```

As you can see, we have added the my_users external pillar with a single argument of [] (empty list).

When Salt loads the modules defined via extension_modules, it is looking for a specifically named method: ext_pillar(). In this particular case, the ext_pillar configuration value is going to make Salt look for *my_users.py* inside the directory */srv/salt/modules* (defined by extension_modules). Inside that file, Salt will execute the method named ext_pillar. After we restart the salt-master service, we should be able to see our new pillar data:

```
[vagrant@master ~]$ sudo salt \* pillar.item my_users
minion3.example:
    ----------
    my_users:
        ----------
        app:
            ----------
            full:
                App User
            uid:
                9001
        barney:
            ----------
            full:
                Barney Rubble
            uid:
                2003
        betty:
            ----------
            full:
                Betty Rubble
            uid:
                2004
        wilma:
            ----------
            full:
                Wilma Flintstone
            uid:
                2001
minion4.example:
    ----------
        my_users:
<snip>
```

This means we can clean up the hardcoded user lists we had defined in the pillar roots. We can combine this user list with some Jinja to significantly simplify our users state. First, let's update the user state itself:

```
[vagrant@master ~]$ cat /srv/salt/file/base/users/init.sls
{% set users = salt['pillar.get']('my_users', {}) %}
{% for login in users.keys() %}
{% set cur_user = users.get(login, {}) %}
{% set uid = cur_user.get('uid', none) %}
{% set full_name = cur_user.get('full', none) %}
```

```
users_{{ login }}:
  user.present:
  - name: {{ login }}
  - fullname: {{ full_name }}
  - uid: {{ uid }}
{% endfor %}

include:
  - .www
```

The users state now pulls the user list and all of the necessary data (like the UID) directly from the pillar data. The first line sets a dictionary to all of the user data we just added via the external pillar. It then simply loops through each value, creates a state ID (e.g., users_wilma), and then sets the rest of the data necessary for the user.present state.

This leads to a significantly simpler top file for our state tree:

```
[vagrant@master ~]$ cat /srv/salt/file/base/top.sls
base:
  '*':
  - default
  - users

  'roles:webserver':
  - match: grain
  - roles.webserver
  - sites
```

Summary

One of the biggest advantages of Salt is that it is very simple to extend many of its parts. We can use a templating language, such as Jinja, to add some basic data manipulations into our states and pillars. But that is just the very beginning of what we can customize. Execution modules lie at the very core of what Salt provides. Writing custom modules means we can add any logic to help us manage our hosts. We can even write custom grains and pillars to add even more advanced logic to our data sources or even query any data source we like. But, again, this is only the beginning of what we can customize. Before we continue, we need to look at some additional capabilities available on the master.

CHAPTER 7

More on the Master

In the previous chapter we started to discuss the various ways that Salt can be extended. But that was just the beginning. Before we can continue, however, we need to take a moment to discuss more details about the master. We have briefly mentioned some of these details, but we need a more concrete foundation before tackling additional ways of extending Salt.

So far we have focused on the master simply coordinating jobs that run on the minions. The master provides data via pillars and serves as a central host from which you can run commands. But up until now, most of the commands have run on the minions themselves. The master has even more power available to you. There are, among others, systems that coordinate multiple jobs in a single command as well as systems that listen to data that comes from the minions.

The first topic we will look at is *runners*. A runner is very similar in concept to an execution module. However, execution modules run on the minions, while runners execute on the master. The minions are isolated and do not have access to much of the Salt infrastructure. The master, on the other hand, has access to everything. This includes all of the minions themselves, the job cache, pillar data, and more. Therefore, a runner can run a command on one minion and, depending on the results from that minion, can then run a different command on other minions.

After we discuss runners, we will discuss a "higher-level" state system. The `orchestrate runner` allows you to define a number of states that run on a single minion, but the results of those states affect the states that follow. This is similar to requisite states, except that a failure in an `orchestrate` runner will affect other minions.

Lastly, we will discuss the *event* system. Salt works by sending messages over a data bus (using ZeroMQ). Other applications can utilize this system to send their own messages. The reactor system allows you to listen for those events (on the master) and then execute commands on the master as a result. This allows the minions to affect the entire Salt system, but only in ways that are predefined.

Runners

The wealth of tools available with grains and modules has proven how powerful Salt can be. But those commands are specific to a single host. Even in small environments, there is almost always a need to coordinate actions across many hosts. For example, you may not want to set up a web server until its corresponding database is ready. *Runners* execute on the master and interact with the master process. Thus, they have access to all of the minions and can handle the kind of coordination with multiple hosts that you will likely need.

Let's explore a very simple runner just to see how it's different from the modules and states we have discussed previously. One of the earliest commands we exposed with execution modules was one to read documentation, sys.doc. There is something similar for runners called doc.runner. As we mentioned back in Chapter 2, runners are called with the salt-run command:

```
[vagrant@master ~]$ sudo salt-run doc.runner
cache.clear_all:

    Clear the cached pillar, grains, and mine data of the targeted minions

    CLI Example:

        salt-run cache.clear_all
<snip>
```

The first thing to notice is that there are no minions listed (i.e., there is no target defined on the command line). *Runners* don't necessarily interact with the minions at all.[1] We are going to introduce a couple of very handy runners: manage and jobs. The manage runner will help show the status of your minions. The second one, jobs, gives us the ability to interact with the job cache. Since the job cache is completely contained on the master, there is no interaction with the minions when we're using the jobs runner. Those two runners show the power of interacting closely with either the minions (as with the manage runner) or something that is totally contained on the master (e.g., the jobs runner).

---

[1] The doc.runner actually does interact with the minions as of version 2015.2.0. This isn't necessary, and that runner should probably be rewritten. It's an important detail if you look at the code, but it doesn't really affect this example.

Manage Minions

The manage runner will give you a number of handy routines to gather information about your minions.

Let's use the manage.up runner to find all of the minions that are up and reporting to the master:

```
[vagrant@master ~]$ sudo salt-run manage.up
master.example
minion1.example
minion2.example
minion3.example
minion4.example
```

One thing should stand out right away: the format is not the same as when we run the salt command. As we mentioned earlier, the salt-run command has no *targets*. You do not list the minions where the command runs because the very definition of a runner is that it runs on the master only. In the case of manage.up, the Salt master simply sends a test.ping out to all minions and reports back all of the minions that respond.

Now, let's look at the manage.down runner. To make it interesting, first disable the Salt minion on the master, then run manage.down:

```
[vagrant@master ~]$ sudo service salt-minion stop
Stopping salt-minion daemon:                          [  OK  ]

[vagrant@master ~]$ sudo salt-run manage.down
master.example
```

In the example with manage.up, things are pretty simple: the Salt master sends out a test.ping to every minion and reports back all of the minions that respond. But in the case of manage.down, how do you know what minions are not available? In this specific case, the manage.down runner uses the list of Salt keys that have been accepted on the master to get a list of all known minions, and then calls manage.up and subtracts the two sets of minions.

Fortunately, there is another runner that combines both actions to give you the "status" of every minion: manage.status:

```
[vagrant@master ~]$ sudo salt-run manage.status
down:
    - master.example
up:
    - minion1.example
    - minion2.example
    - minion3.example
    - minion4.example
```

Don't forget to start the `salt-minion` daemon back up:

```
[vagrant@master ~]$ sudo service salt-minion start
Starting salt-minion daemon:                        [  OK  ]
```

The takeaway here is that since runners run only on the master, you can utilize all of the functionality available on the master. In the case of the `manage.down` and `manage.status` runners, they use the data available in Salt's key lists to determine the state of every minion. Also, you can interact with all of Salt's modules and states to grab information from the minions. With the `manage.up` runner, the `test.ping` module is used to determine which minions are available.

Manage Jobs

When we run code using the `salt` command, a *job* is posted to the pub-sub bus (via ZeroMQ) and the minions will respond to that job. But if there are a lot of people running commands against a number of minions, how does the master keep all of that data straight? Simply put, the master creates a *job ID* when the command is sent to ZeroMQ. The minions will then include that ID when responding back to the master. The jobs runners make it easier to look at jobs.

A common use of the `jobs` runners is to look at the status of a job that is taking a long time to complete. We can simulate a slow-running job using the `test.sleep` module.

Let's run `test.sleep` with a value of `20`. Then, let's Ctrl-C out of the command:

```
[vagrant@master ~]$ sudo salt \* test.sleep 20
^CExiting on Ctrl-C
This job's jid is:
20150226174911628089
The minions may not have all finished running and any remaining minions
will return upon completion. To look up the return data for this job
later run:
salt-run jobs.lookup_jid 20150226174911628089
```

When a `salt` command exits prematurely, it will give the user the value of the job ID so that any return data can be examined later. It's important to remember that even if the command exits (either by exceeding the timeout or by being forcibly quit) the master process will continue to receive data from the minions and record it.

In the preceding example, the job ID (`jid`) is given to the user, along with the exact command to use to examine any data returned by that job. If we run that exact command again, but this time *also* run the Salt runner `jobs.lookup_jid`, we can see the data available in the jobs cache:

```
[vagrant@master ~]$ sudo salt \* test.sleep 20
^CExiting on Ctrl-C
This job's jid is:
20150226175035298308
```

```
The minions may not have all finished running and any remaining minions
will return upon completion. To look up the return data for this job
later run:
salt-run jobs.lookup_jid 20150226175035298308
```

Wait 20 seconds for the preceding command to complete, and then you should see
the data returned from that job:

```
[vagrant@master ~]$ sudo salt-run jobs.lookup_jid 20150226175035298308
master.example:
    True
minion1.example:
    True
minion2.example:
    True
minion3.example:
    True
minion4.example:
    True
```

Try rerunning the command, but with a higher sleep time. Then query the job cache
(with jobs.lookup_jid) right away:

```
[vagrant@master ~]$ sudo salt \* test.sleep 100
^CExiting on Ctrl-C
This job's jid is:
20150226175421153996
The minions may not have all finished running and any remaining minions
will return upon completion. To look up the return data for this job
later run:
salt-run jobs.lookup_jid 20150226175421153996
[vagrant@master ~]$ sudo salt-run jobs.lookup_jid 20150226175421153996
[vagrant@master ~]$
```

The jobs.lookup_jid command didn't return any data. What happened?

Remember, the job cache has the return data from the minions. The goal of the
jobs.lookup_jid runner is to display that return data. If you did not see anything
come back (as in the example), then it is likely you didn't wait long enough for the
minions to finish the command; in this case, you didn't wait 100 seconds for the command to complete and return data to the master. If you wait a minute or two and run
it again, you will likely see the following:

```
[vagrant@master ~]$ sudo salt-run jobs.lookup_jid 20150226175421153996
master.example:
    True
minion1.example:
    True
minion2.example:
    True
minion3.example:
    True
```

```
minion4.example:
    True
```

This all assumes you know the job ID with your data. There is a `jobs.list_jobs` runner that will show all of the jobs that are still in the job cache:

```
[vagrant@master ~]$ sudo salt-run jobs.list_jobs
20150226174108241385:
    ----------
    Arguments:
    Function:
        test.ping
    StartTime:
        2015, Feb 26 17:41:08.241385
    Target:
        *
    Target-type:
        glob
    User:
        sudo_vagrant
20150226174113251518:
    ----------
<snip>
```

The format of the output should be pretty clear. The first line contains the job ID, followed by the Salt module called, when the module was started, and so on.

 The Salt master keeps only a limited number of jobs in the job cache. The default is 24 hours. This value can be modified, but you should be careful when changing it. If you go too high, the jobs runner can take a very long time to run because of all of the data it has to search. If it's too low, the master may clean out job data for jobs that have not completed.

The orchestrate Runner

We have seen how useful the state system is for managing a number of hosts, but so far, we've only worked with a single host at a time. There is a feature in Salt for managing state runs across multiple minions: the `orchestrate` runner.

The basic format of orchestration SLS files is almost the same as a standard state (SLS) file. However, since the execution action may span hosts and may need to be coordinated among hosts, we need a centralized process to manage the actions. This is the very definition of a runner. The main command is `state.orchestrate`, and as with all runners, we need to run it using the `salt-run` command, not the `salt` command. While the basic formats of the SLS files are nearly the same, since they are controlled via a runner, they need to know which minions to act upon. So, the orchestration SLS files have a `target` attribute, similar to the top file (*top.sls*).

You may see references to the OverState runner. That has been deprecated as of this writing and will be removed in a future release. But all of the functionality available in the OverState runner is provided via the orchestrate runner.

Earlier, we showed how to update the version of the web software. We did this with a state file: sites. Now, we want to make sure the database is updated first. If the database update should fail, then we want the web servers to remain at their current version of the software:

```
[vagrant@master ~]$ cat /srv/salt/file/base/orch/web.sls
{% set myenv = 'stage' %}
data_update:
  salt.state:
  - tgt: 'G@roles:database and G@myenv:{{ myenv }}'
  - tgt_type: compound
  - sls: database.update

web_update:
  salt.state:
  - tgt: 'G@roles:webserver and G@myenv:{{ myenv }}'
  - tgt_type: compound
  - sls: roles.webserver
  - require:
    - salt: data_update
```

As you can see, we are using the require clause to make sure the database update runs first. Again, since it is a runner, the SLS file needs to have the targeting information available:

```
[vagrant@master ~]$ sudo salt-run state.orchestrate orch.web
master.example_master:
  ---------
          ID: data_update
    Function: salt.state
      Result: True
     Comment: States ran successfully. Updating minion3.example.
     Started: 04:47:26.664236
    Duration: 2239.498 ms
     Changes:
              minion3.example:
                ----------
                        ID: database_update
                  Function: file.managed
                      Name: /tmp/data.txt
                    Result: True
                   Comment: File /tmp/data.txt updated
                   Started: 04:47:28.536697
                  Duration: 14.715 ms
                   Changes:
```

```
                         - - - - - - - - - -
                         diff:
                                 New file

            Summary
            - - - - - - - - - - -
            Succeeded: 1 (changed=1)
            Failed:    0
            - - - - - - - - - - -
            Total states run:       1
     - - - - - - - - -
             ID: web_update
       Function: salt.state
         Result: True
        Comment: States ran successfully.
        Started: 04:47:28.904207
       Duration: 190.568 ms
        Changes:

Summary
- - - - - - - - - - -
Succeeded: 2 (changed=1)
Failed:    0
- - - - - - - - - - -
Total states run:       2
```

The Event System

The event system is at the very core of how Salt communicates. The minions will send
events (via the ZeroMQ pub-sub interface) and the master will react to those events.
You have complete access to the event system. You can view other events as they come
into the master, or you can even fire your own events. Before we start sending our
own events, however, let's look at the basic structure of an event.

Events are very simple data structures. There is an ID for every message and then its
corresponding data. The name or ID of the event is called the tag. The format of the
tag looks very similar to that of a file in a filesystem. It is a hierarchical format where
the different levels are separated by slashes. Just as in a filesystem, each level of the *tag*
represents an increasingly specific namespace. All communication by Salt itself is
namespaced with a leading *salt/* in the *tag*. More levels follow, each separated by a
slash (*/*), just like in a filesystem.

We will only be discussing the format of the events in the context of Salt itself. However, Salt uses standard open source software in its core. The communication between the hosts is over ZeroMQ, as we have discussed. In addition, the messages are serialized using *msgpack* (*http://msgpack.org/*). This is why we don't discuss looking at the messages in *raw ZeroMQ* format. This is certainly possible, but it is beyond the scope of this book.

As an example, after the master has sent a job to the minion and the minion has performed whatever action is needed, the minion will return data to the master. The tag for the event returned to the master would look like:

```
salt/job/20141201051607849201/ret/minion1.example
```

If we break that down, we would see the following:

```
top level: salt
next level: job
job ID: 20141201051607849201
type: ret (return data)
minion ID: minion1.example
```

By namespacing all of Salt's internal events to begin with `salt`, you can more easily write custom events that will not interfere with any Salt events. Also, if you want to perform your own actions based on Salt's events, there is a clean format that you can learn.

The second part of the event data structure is the data itself. This is simply a Python dictionary. For example, a very simple data portion of an event would look like the following:

```
'{some_key: the_value}'
```

Now, let's send an event from a minion to the master. The simplest way to fire your own event is using the command `event.send`. Since we are running it on the minion itself, we will need to use the `salt-call` command:

```
[vagrant@minion1 ~]$ sudo salt-call event.send example/test \
'{my_key: some_value}'
local:
    True
```

The arguments should be pretty straightforward: first the tag and then the data. Also, `salt-call` returns a `True` value to let you know the command succeeded.

If you are watching the Salt master's log, and you have the log level set to `DEBUG`, you should see something like the following in the log:

```
2015-04-13 03:59:17,903 [salt.utils.event][DEBUG    ]
Sending event - data = {'tgt_type': 'glob', 'fun_args': ['example/test',
'{my_key: some_value}'], 'jid': '20150413035917901437', 'return': True,
```

```
'retcode': 0, 'success': True, 'tgt': 'minion1.example', 'cmd': '_return',
'_stamp': '2015-04-13T03:59:17.903245', 'arg': ['example/test',
'{my_key: some_value}'], 'fun': 'event.send', 'id': 'minion1.example'}
```

Being able to send messages using the exact same data bus as Salt uses gives us a wealth of power to extend Salt even more. In the next section, we will discuss how you can run commands when jobs match a pattern, using the *reactor system*.

The Reactor System

We have just discussed how the various Salt pieces talk to each other using the event system. The *reactor* system allows us to perform custom actions on the master when a certain event comes in. The reactor is broken up into two parts. The first part is associating the various events with actions to be performed. The association is with the event's tag mapping to a list of SLS files. These SLS files are specific to the reactor. The second part of the reactor is setting up the actions in the SLS file.

First, we need to add the mapping of the event's tag to an SLS file. This is done in the master's configuration. Let's create a file specifically for this purpose:

```
[vagrant@master ~]$ cat /etc/salt/master.d/reactor.conf
reactor:
- 'example/*':
  - /srv/salt/reactor/track_example.sls
```

This should be pretty obvious: take any event that has a tag with a top-level namespace of example and execute the *track_example.sls* file.

Let's record the data into a file so we can see what's happening:

```
[vagrant@master ~]$ cat /srv/salt/reactor/track_example.sls
track_example_tag:
  local.file.append:
  - tgt: master.example
  - arg:
    - /tmp/reactor_example.txt
    - {{ data }}
```

Just like in state files, Salt will expose custom variables (via Jinja) to the SLS file. We are simply echoing all of the data to a file.

If we send an event via event.send, as before we should see our data get appended into */tmp/reactor_example.txt*. First, since the example uses file.append, we need to create the file:

```
[vagrant@master ~]$ touch /tmp/reactor_example.txt
```

Then we use salt-call event.send:

```
[vagrant@minion1 ~]$ sudo salt-call event.send \
     example/test '{my_key: some_value}'
local:
    True

[vagrant@master ~]$ cat /tmp/reactor_example.txt
{'_stamp': '2015-04-13T04:10:53.830594', 'pretag': 'None',
'cmd': '_minion_event', 'tag': 'example/test', 'data': {'__pub_fun':
'event.send', '__pub_pid': 4017, '__pub_jid': '20150413041053408567',
'my_key': 'some_value', '__pub_tgt': 'salt-call'},
'id': 'minion1.example'}
```

Also, we should see the event data and the subsequent call to the reactor system in the Salt master logs:

```
2015-04-13 04:10:54,215 [salt.utils.event][DEBUG    ] Sending event -
data = {'fun_args': ['/tmp/reactor_example.txt', {'_stamp':
2015-04-13T04:10:53.830594', 'pretag': 'None', 'cmd': '_minion_event',
'tag': 'example/test', 'data': {'__pub_fun': 'event.send', 'my_key':
'some_value', '__pub_jid': '20150413041053408567', '__pub_pid': 4017,
'__pub_tgt': 'salt-call'}, 'id': 'minion1.example'}], 'jid':
'20150413041053960830', 'return': 'Wrote 1 lines to
"/tmp/reactor_example.txt"', 'retcode': 0, 'success': True, 'cmd':
'_return', '_stamp': '2015-04-13T04:10:54.215204', 'fun': 'file.append',
'id': 'master.example'}

2015-04-13 04:10:54,216 [salt.utils.event][DEBUG    ] Sending event -
data = {'fun_args': ['/tmp/reactor_example.txt', {'_stamp':
'2015-04-13T04:10:53.830594', 'pretag': 'None', 'cmd': '_minion_event',
'tag': 'example/test', 'data': {'__pub_fun': 'event.send', 'my_key':
'some_value', '__pub_jid': '20150413041053408567', '__pub_pid': 4017,
'__pub_tgt': 'salt-call'}, 'id': 'minion1.example'}], 'jid':
'20150413041053960830', 'return': 'Wrote 1 lines to
"/tmp/reactor_example.txt"', 'retcode': 0, 'success': True, 'cmd':
'_return', '_stamp': '2015-04-13T04:10:54.215523', 'fun': 'file.append',
'id': 'master.example'}
```

The reactor is very powerful, but you should be careful not to over-extend it. As of this writing, the reactor is single-threaded. So, you will want to make the previous SLS example as fast and lightweight as possible. You want to keep your reactor execution simple so you don't tie up necessary resources. Note, this is for the reactor piece specifically; the state function that is called can be long-running.

Summary

The Salt master does more than just coordinate the running of execution or state modules among its minions; it also offers higher-level abstractions where you can programmatically control more of your infrastructure. The *event system* allows you to send messages using the same encrypted communication system that the rest of Salt uses. *Runners* offer a way to execute code specific to the master. The code can give you more insight into the various data elements on the master (such as the job cache), or can communicate with your minions just like the `salt` command does. Lastly, the `orchestrate` runner allows you to create abstractions using the state system where the command coordination needs to span multiple minions. These systems allow you to tie together many of the minion-specific systems to give you more power over all of your systems as a whole.

CHAPTER 8

Extending Salt: Part II

We saw earlier how to extend Salt via custom states, modules, and grains. But we can customize so much more. In this chapter, we will look at the basics of what is available with the Python client API. With this API, you can write standalone Python scripts that call into the Salt infrastructure. We will also touch on how to write custom runners.

Python Client API

The Python client API allows you to interact with the Salt code at a much deeper level than we have seen thus far. There are many ways to import the Salt code into your own Python scripts. However, using the client API will make sure the infrastructure is called properly. For example, the client API will make sure access control lists (ACLs) are not bypassed. We are going to discuss how to write scripts to mimic behavior on both the master (using the LocalClient API) and the minion (using the Caller API). First, though, we need to mention the configuration calls.

Reading Configuration Data on a Master and Minion

There are two primary methods for reading configuration data: `client_config` and `minion_config`. The latter should be obvious; it's used on a minion to parse the minion's configuration files. The former, `client_config`, is actually for reading and parsing the configuration files for the Salt master. They both return dictionaries. They are not always required, but using them will give you more insight into what data the other APIs need.

As we mentioned, the `client_config` is actually used to read the configuration for the master. The API call will make sure all of the files in *master.d* are read as well as making sure the proper defaults are assigned. Also, since it simply reads the configuration files, it does not require the Salt master to be running. A very simple example would be listing the ports used by the master:

```
[vagrant@master ~]$ cat /srv/salt/scripts/show-master-ports.py
#!/usr/bin/env python
import salt.config
_MASTER_CONFIG_FILE = '/etc/salt/master'
master_config = salt.config.client_config(_MASTER_CONFIG_FILE)
print 'Return port: {0}'.format(master_config.get('ret_port'))
print 'Publish port: {0}'.format(master_config.get('publish_port'))

$ /srv/salt/misc/show-master-ports.py
Return port: 4506
Publish port: 4505
```

Since all of the Salt configuration files are just YAML files, you can add your own configuration. As long as you don't use an existing key and you are using valid YAML, you can add more data to the configuration for your own use. Let's add a simple configuration file to the *master.d* directory:

```
[vagrant@master ~]$ cat /etc/salt/master.d/custom.conf
my_custom:
    first_key: this is the first key
    second_key: this is the other key (#2)
```

 Remember that the salt master will read all of the files matching *.conf in /etc/salt/master.d. You can change the default behavior by modifying the configuration key default_include:. The location is relative to the main master configuration file. If you want to add other files, perhaps in other locations in the filesystem, you can use the include: directive.

Then we can write a script very similar to the preceding one and extract that data:

```
[vagrant@master ~]$ cat /srv/salt/scripts/show-custom.py
#!/usr/bin/env python

import salt.config

_MASTER_CONFIG_FILE = '/etc/salt/master'

master_config = salt.config.client_config(_MASTER_CONFIG_FILE)

print 'Custom data: {0}'.format(master_config.get('my_custom'))
[vagrant@master ~]$ /srv/salt/misc/show-custom.py
Custom data:
        {'second_key': 'this is the other key (#2)',
         'first_key': 'this is the first key'}
```

The use of the minion_config routine is almost identical:

```
[vagrant@master ~]$ cat /srv/salt/scripts/show-master.py
#!/usr/bin/env python

import salt.config

_MINION_CONFIG_FILE = '/etc/salt/minion'

minion_config = salt.config.minion_config(_MINION_CONFIG_FILE)

print 'Master: {0}'.format(minion_config.get('master'))
[vagrant@master ~]$ /srv/se-book/example-data/extend-2/show-master.py
Master: 172.31.0.11
```

 I (Craig) used the preceding technique to manage the configuration of *out-of-band* scripts—specifically, scripts that gathered metrics about each minion and reported back to a centralized service.

All of the minions had to have (slightly) custom configurations. Since the minion's configuration files were already managed by another application, it was simple to add further configuration.

Using the Master Client (LocalClient) API

The LocalClient (aka the *master client*) API includes a number of different methods. While we are only going to explore the cmd method here, be aware that there are several others. For example, the batch method will send a command in batches to the minions. This is very handy if you will be calling a script often and you have concerns about overwhelming the master. The remaining methods are well documented, and the following example should give you a sufficient background to explore the other methods.

We are going to call out to all of the minions and get a list of all of the users on each system. But rather than display all of them, we are going to show only those that start with the letter *a*:

```
[vagrant@master ~]$ cat /srv/salt/scripts/user-list.py
#!/usr/bin/env python

import getpass
import logging
import sys
import salt.client
import salt.log

salt.log.setup_console_logger()
logger = logging.getLogger(__name__)
logger.setLevel(logging.WARN)

try:
```

```
    master_client = salt.client.LocalClient()
    all_users = master_client.cmd('*', 'user.list_users')
except salt.exceptions.EauthAuthenticationError:
    logger.fatal('Could not authenitcate with master.')
    cur_user = getpass.getuser()
    if cur_user != 'root':
        logger.fatal('Trying running as root (sudo).')
    sys.exit(1)

for min in all_users:
    print min
    for user in all_users[min]:
        if user.startswith('a'):
            print "  ", user
```

We'll start at the top with the imported modules. The one required for the Local Client is salt.client. This is where all of the client API code is centralized. Next, you'll see the initialization of the logging module and then the subsequent call to set up the console logger. You can simply create your own logger instance, if you prefer. However, the salt.client code will create its own handlers if there are none present. This can make it a little difficult to get logging working. Using salt.log.setup_con sole_logger() will make that much simpler.

 Since we are writing a script to interact with the Salt system, and not extending Salt **itself**, the logging messages in the script will *not* be seen in the master's logs. This may or may not be what you want. Just be aware of it.

The important part is the initialization of the LocalClient object. There are no required arguments. However, if you have your configuration data somewhere other than */etc/salt/master*, you will need to pass that in via a keyword argument: c_path. Next, there is a call to the cmd method. The format is pretty simple:

```
First argument: minion targeting string (*)
Second Argument: module to run (user.list_users)
```

Any additional arguments required by the module call would be in the third and fourth positions. In the third position would be a list of positional arguments required by the module. For example, a call to the cmd.run module would look like:

```
master_client.cmd('*', 'cmd.run', ['uptime'])
```

If there are any keyword arguments, they would be put into a dictionary and placed in the fourth position.

Next, you'll see the exception handling for authentication errors. The different client APIs will adhere to whatever ACLs you have in place. In our example, only root can run commands. If we were to run the previous example as an unprivileged user, we would raise that exception:

```
[vagrant@master ~]$ /srv/salt/misc/user-list.py
[CRITICAL] Could not authenitcate with master.
[CRITICAL] Trying running as root (sudo).
```

However, running it as root, we get the output we were looking for:

```
[vagrant@master ~]$ sudo /srv/se-book/example-data/extend-2/user-list.py
minion4.example
minion3.example
minion2.example
    adm
minion1.example
    adm
master.example
    adm
```

Remember, we have a couple of Ubuntu hosts, while the others are CentOS. That is why they did not all return the same data. While this example is slightly contrived, it does show the power of the LocalClient API. If you cannot quite figure out how to either target or parse the output in a way you like, the LocalClient API will allow you to do whatever you need in Python itself.

Using the Caller Client API

The LocalClient API is great for running more code on the master, but if you need to run something that interacts with the minion, then the Caller client API is what you need. The Caller client uses the same interfaces as the salt-call CLI, and it is much simpler than the LocalClient. The only method we are going to discuss here is function. The format looks very similar to the preceding LocalClient example. For this example, let's get a list of all of the grains that begin with os:

```
[vagrant@master ~]$ cat /srv/salt/scripts/caller-example.py
#!/usr/bin/env python

import logging
import salt.client
import salt.log

salt.log.setup_console_logger()
logger = logging.getLogger(__name__)
logger.setLevel(logging.WARN)

salt_client = salt.client.Caller()
grains = salt_client.function('grains.items')

for grain in grains:
    if grain.startswith('os'):
        print 'Key {0} = {1}'.format(grain, grains.get(grain))
```

Running it on the master gives us:

```
[vagrant@master ~]$ sudo /srv/salt/misc/caller-example.py
Key osrelease = 6.6
Key osfinger = CentOS-6
Key osmajorrelease = 6
Key osfullname = CentOS
Key os_family = RedHat
Key oscodename = Final
Key osarch = x86_64
Key osrelease_info = (6, 6)
Key os = CentOS
```

This should all look very familiar. Again, we start out by importing the `salt.client` module, and `salt.log` and `logging` to handle the logging aspects. Next, we initialize the Salt client. Then, we call the `function` method with a single argument: the name of the Salt module we want to execute.

The exception handling for authentication was left out for brevity. It is just as important for the Caller client as for LocalClient, however.

You might recall when we first discussed the `salt-call` CLI, there was an option to *not* talk back to the master. We can replicate that behavior here, but we need to amend the basic configuration options. We'll have to read in the minion configuration and then add a directive to tell the API to make only local calls:

```
[vagrant@master ~]$ cat /srv/salt/scripts/caller-local-example.py
#!/usr/bin/env python

import logging
import salt.client
import salt.log
import salt.config

min_config = salt.config.minion_config('/etc/salt/minion')

min_config['file_client'] = 'local'

salt.log.setup_console_logger()
logger = logging.getLogger(__name__)
logger.setLevel(logging.WARN)

salt_client = salt.client.Caller(mopts=min_config)
grains = salt_client.function('grains.items')

for grain in grains:
```

```
if grain.startswith('os'):
    print 'Key {0} = {1}'.format(grain, grains.get(grain))
```

The big difference is that we set the `file_client` key to `local`. That is the equivalent of running `salt-call --local`.

The preceding code is only a very small taste of what you can do with the Python client API. There is a significant number of additional customizations available. Next we will cover writing a custom runner and look at one additional API, the Runner-Client.

Custom Runners

Earlier, you learned that we execute a runner on the master using the `salt-run` CLI command. A runner can gather data from a number of minions (as we saw with the various `manage` runner functions), or it can simply look at data available only on the master (as we saw with the `jobs` runner functions). In this section we will explore two different options for using the runner libraries: writing a custom runner and utilizing the RunnerClient Python API.

Writing a Custom Runner

Runners are great for *command and control*. Since they run on the master, they can communicate to any minion connected to that master and then munge the data in any way you need. As we stated earlier, the `salt-run` command does not take a target as an argument, unlike the `salt` command. It is up to the code within the runner itself to determine which, if any, minion it needs to communicate with. We just introduced the LocalClient API, and now we are going to use it in our runner.

First, however, we need to add a configuration variable to our master. When we introduced runners, we just used the ones that are a part of Salt. Now that we want to write our own, we need to tell the Salt master where to find these files. We will add a file, *runner.conf*, to the standard *master.d* configuration directory:

```
[vagrant@master ~]$ sudo cat /etc/salt/master.d/runner.conf
runner_dirs:
- /srv/salt/runner
```

As always, we need to restart the master for the configuration to be active.[1]

Now, let's add a simple runner:

---

1 This step is a bit redundant since we set the configuration option `extension_modules` in "External Pillars" on page 102. If we wanted to use that setting, then our custom runners would be located at */srv/salt/modules/runners*.

```
[vagrant@master ~]$ cat /srv/salt/runner/monitor.py
#!/usr/bin/env python

import salt.client

def procs(num_procs_raw):
    '''
    Show any minions that are above a certain number of processes.
    '''
    master_client = salt.client.LocalClient()
    num_procs = int(num_procs_raw)
    all_procs = master_client.cmd('*', 'cmd.run', ['ps -e | wc -l'])
    for minion in all_procs.keys():
        cur_procs = int(all_procs[minion])
        if cur_procs > num_procs:
            print 'Minion {0}: {1} > {2}'.format(minion, cur_procs, num_procs)
```

Just as with the earlier example, we create an instance of LocalClient and then use the cmd method to run our commands on the minions of interest. Again, we are targeting all minions (*). You'll notice that the method definition has an argument defined. Salt will make sure that any positional arguments defined in your method are entered when salt-run is called:

```
[vagrant@master ~]$ sudo salt-run monitor.procs 80
Minion minion1.example: 81 > 80
Minion master.example: 108 > 80
```

The argument passed in to the salt-run command is then relayed to the runner code. Salt will ensure that any arguments are available. Here's a quick example of what happens when the argument is left out:

```
[vagrant@master ~]$ sudo salt-run monitor.procs
[ERROR   ] An un-handled exception was caught by salt's global exception handler:
TypeError: procs() takes exactly 1 argument (0 given)
Traceback (most recent call last):
  File "/usr/bin/salt-run", line 10, in <module>
    salt_run()
<snip>
```

If you have optional arguments, you can add them as keyword arguments.

The preceding example doesn't seem that much different from the example of using LocalClient directly. However, when you use the runner system, you have access to a number of Salt's internal data structures. Just as with custom modules, you can *cross-call* other Salt routines using the salt dictionary. Also, configuration variables are available in the opts dictionary. Let's look at a way we can combine optional keyword arguments with the dictionaries that Salt provides:

```
[vagrant@master ~]$ cat /srv/salt/runners/vars.py
#!/usr/bin/env python

def show(match=None):
    '''
    Show the various runner data structures.
    '''
    if match:
        print 'Matching: {0}'.format(match)
        for opt in __opts__.keys():
            if match in opt:
                print 'Option found: {0}'.format(opt)
        for cmd in __salt__.keys():
            if match in cmd:
                print 'Command found: {0}'.format(cmd)
    else:
        print 'Showing all.'
        for opt in __opts__.keys():
            print opt
        for cmd in __salt__.keys():
            print cmd
```

As you can see, we added a keyword argument (match) to the method definition.[2] If that value is present, the runner will print all commands and configuration keys that match it:

```
[vagrant@master ~]$ sudo salt-run vars.show match=stat
Matching: stat
Option found: state_auto_order
Option found: state_verbose
Option found: state_aggregate
Option found: state_events
Option found: state_output
Option found: state_top
Command found: state.orch
Command found: state.show_stages
Command found: state.over
Command found: state.sls
Command found: state.orchestrate
Command found: state.event
Command found: manage.status
```

Next, let's look at how we can use the RunnerClient API from the Python client API.

---

2 The print statements will be redundant in version 2015.2.

Using the RunnerClient API

We can use the RunnerClient API to call any runner. The API should look familiar at
this point. One key difference is that it requires the master configuration data to be
passed in:

```
#!/usr/bin/env python

import salt.runner
import salt.config

master_opts = salt.config.client_config('/etc/salt/master')
run_client = salt.runner.RunnerClient(master_opts)

jobs = run_client.cmd('jobs.list_jobs', [])

for job_id in jobs:
    job_data = jobs[job_id]
    print '{0} started at: {1}'.format(job_id, job_data['StartTime'])


$ sudo /srv/salt/misc/job-start.py
20141215050313918564 started at: 2014, Dec 15 05:03:13.918564
20141215000645762060 started at: 2014, Dec 15 00:06:45.762060
20141215064445473318 started at: 2014, Dec 15 06:44:45.473318
<snip>
```

Summary

Salt provides a variety of ways for us to extend it and to call into it using various APIs.
We have introduced only a few very basic examples so you can have a rough idea of
what is possible. There is a great deal more to explore, and we hope these examples
inspire you to experiment with the other APIs and methods you can use to increase
Salt's power.

CHAPTER 9

Topology and Configuration Options

The majority of this book has focused on the various ways to use and extend Salt using a single master controlling multiple minions. But there are other configurations that give you a great deal of flexibility. Before getting into different topologies, let's look at some of the options in the master configuration.

Master Configuration

The configuration for the master has many options. However, this book is not meant to cover every one in detail. There are a few options in particular that you need to understand when learning to use Salt.

Directories and Files

Over the previous chapters, we have mentioned various directories used on the master. These directories were necessary to understand in order to extend Salt itself. There are a few other directories that, most likely, you will not need to modify, but it is important to know of them and roughly what they do (see Table 9-1).

Table 9-1. Additional directories used on the master

Option key	Summary
root_dir	The base directory that is prepended to most other directories.
pki_dir	The directory that contains all of the minion and master keys. Since it contains both private and public keys, be careful of the permissions.
cachedir	The directory where the job data is stored.

Option key	Summary
sock_dir	The location of the sockets that Salt uses in its communication channels.
log_file	The location of the master's log.

There are a few scenarios where you may want to detour from the defaults—for example, if you want all of your Salt master configuration and all of its data on a separate disk volume. The *pki_dir* and the *cachedir* directories will have a fair number of reads and writes. If you are having performance problems, you may want to explore moving those directories to a faster disk. There are some serious pros and cons with doing so, however. For example, if you move *cachedir* to a RAM-backed filesystem (e.g., *tmpfs*), and your master reboots, you will lose all of your job data. By default, however, the master keeps only 24 hours of history, so this may be an acceptable compromise. Going into a great deal of detail about the strengths and weaknesses of various approaches is really beyond the scope of this book, but it is important that you are aware of the aforementioned directories and files.

Logging

Throughout the book we have referred to various entries in the logfiles. The default location of the master and minion logs is in */var/log/salt/master* and */var/log/salt/minion*, respectively. The default logging levels are set to warning. As with many systems, you can alter these log levels to anything from debug to critical.

There are two additional levels below debug: garbage and trace. Setting your logs to debug will generate quite a few messages and should contain any pertinent details. Be aware that there are additional, and uncommon, levels to provide even more information. They are typically used in development when one needs to see all of those details.

One of the most important pieces of the logging configuration is that you can have different levels for *console* and *file* logging. As a result, you may see different messages in Salt's logfile as opposed to what is seen on the console. (By *console*, we mean whatever system is tracking that output. It may be the system that controls system daemons—e.g., upstart—or any other process control system.) If you change either one, it may be best to change the other, just to minimize confusion. The configuration options you should search for are: log_level (for the console logs) and log_level_logfile.

Next, you do not have to log directly to the filesystem. The format of the log_file option allows for a URI. Specifically, the option can have a leading protocol: file, tcp, or udp. Thus, you can ship your logs off to a centralized system for parsing, recording, or whatever you need.

Obviously, changing the logging level will alter the number of messages that are recorded. But you can also change the format of those messages. This can come in very handy if you need to centralize your logs and your system expects a very specific format. There are two different pairs of format configuration options: one for the date format and another for the body format. It should come as no surprise that the options for modifying the date formats are `log_datefmt` and `log_datefmt_logfile`. These options will accept standard `strftime` parameters. (For example, `%Y` gives the four-digit year, while `%y` will give the two-digit year. You can easily search for `strftime` to find a complete list.) To modify the body, you have the options `log_fmt_console` and `log_fmt_logfile`. These use the standard Python logging format attributes. (For example, *%(levelname)* will give the log level: debug, info, etc.) In addition, Salt has added a few other options to help colorize the console log output:

- %(colorlevel)
- %(colorname)
- %(colorprocess)
- %(colormsg)

The preceding options allow you to change logging output, but at a relatively coarse level. There is an additional option for more fine-grained logging: `log_granular_lev els`. As the name suggests, this allows you to set different parts of the Salt system to different levels.

For example, if you need to debug why a module is not behaving as intended, but do not want to get swamped by, say, authentication messages, you can add the following:

```
log_granular_levels:
    'salt': 'warning'
    'salt.modules': 'debug'
```

Access Control

All of the examples have called the `salt` command either directly as the `root` user or via `sudo`. However, there is an access control system that gives you more control. There are two aspects: a whitelist and a blacklist. The whitelist will allow users to run the `salt` command as themselves, while the blacklist will restrict access. You can specify only the users and which commands they can and cannot run. You cannot, for example, give a list of hosts for which they can run commands. (A little later, we will discuss the peer system, which does have such a capability.)

The whitelist, or `client_acl` option, can be used to allow non-root users to run the Salt command. However, you have to change the permissions on several directories:

```
$ sudo chmod 755
    /var/cache/salt \
    /var/cache/salt/master \
    /var/cache/salt/master/jobs \
    /var/run/salt \
    /var/run/salt/master
```

When running the `salt` command, you need access to the cache files (`cachedir`), the job data, and the socket files in the *run* directory (`sockdir`). In addition, you will likely need to write to the logfiles. This means changing the master log to be writable by the users who are running the `salt` command. One way to handle this situation is to create a group that has write access to the master's logfile (*/var/log/salt/master*). However, the `client_acl` supports only a list of users, so you will need to keep those two lists in sync with each other.

Here's a simple `client_acl` example:

```
client_acl:
  vagrant:
    - test.*
```

Now you should be able to run `salt * test.ping` as the `vagrant` user. The format is a user key followed by a list of commands that can be run by that user. (The command definition is a regular expression and not a simple wildcard.)

The `client_acl_blacklist` will do the opposite: restrict certain users or certain commands:

```
client_acl_blacklist:
  users:
    - root
    - '^(?!sudo_).*$'   # all non sudo users
  modules:
    - cmd
```

The format is slightly different than with the `client_acl`. Since you can limit either users or commands, there are two sections to configure each independently. In the `users` section, there is a list of users who will be blocked. Just as with `client_acl`, the list is a list of regular expressions, not just strings. This is obvious with the second user. The second user will block any username that does not start with `sudo`. This will force users to run the `salt` command using `sudo` and not getting a root shell.

Running `salt` commands as `root` directly has a lot of appeal since it is far simpler. However, it creates difficulties because the logs won't reflect the ID of a real user who executed a command. When things go wrong, you really need to find out who did what so you can get all of the right people together to fix whatever broke. This is far easier when the logs show the real user ID that ran every command.

In the `modules` section, you see only `cmd`. The `cmd` module is very handy, but also very dangerous. Salt provides a lot of power. If you run `rm -rf /` on a single host, that's bad enough. However, if you run it with `salt` on every host you have, that could make for a very long and difficult day. The beauty of Salt is that if you do need to remove every file in a directory, you can write a simple module for that. In that module, you can check to make sure that `/` is not the argument given. However, restricting any command may not work in your infrastructure. The preceding example simply shows what has been done at other places.

The ACLs just listed are specifically for the `salt` command, not the entire Salt system. This *only* forbids users from using that command via the `salt` CLI, but *does* allow that command in, say, states. For example, in the case of the `client_acl_blacklist` we limited the use of the `cmd` module. But if there is an SLS file that uses the `cmd` module, then that state could still be run/used.

File Server Options

The file server built in to Salt is used by a large section of Salt, including the state system and the modules. We touched on the multiple file roots and breaking them into different environments. But all of these files came off the local disk on the Salt master. Salt can also query external sources for files. Namely, Salt can talk to Git, Subversion, and Mercurial. They all have very similar functionality, but some are more developed than others. Also, the nature of each system will lend itself better or worse to some features. We will show an example using the Git backend.

As we discussed earlier, the file roots are broken up into multiple environments. Minions can get access to each environment via the *top file*. Using the Git file server, you can map these environments to Git branches. The first step is to enable the Git file server by adding it to the `fileserver_backend` option:

```
[vagrant@master ~]$ cat /etc/salt/master.d/git.conf
fileserver_backend:
- roots
- git
```

This will tell Salt to look in both the local files and in the Git file server. In order to minimize issues with third parties, we will use a Git server on the Salt master itself.

 We are running the Git server on the Salt master simply for convenience. In a production setup, you should carefully consider if this is wise. While it makes a number of things easier (e.g., all of the code necessary for the master to work properly lives on the master), it does present some security challenges.

To make things easier on ourselves, we are going to create a state to manage the master itself. The first thing we will add is a Git directory:

```
[vagrant@master srv]$ cat /srv/salt/file/base/top.sls
base:
  '*':
  - default
  - users

  'roles:webserver':
  - match: grain
  - roles.webserver
  - sites

  'master.example':
  - master

[vagrant@master srv]$ cat /srv/salt/file/base/master/init.sls
include:
- .git-dir
[vagrant@master srv]$ cat /srv/salt/file/base/master/git-dir.sls
master_git_dir:
  file.directory:
  - name: /srv/git
  - user: root
```

We just added a target in the top file for our master (`master.example`) and then added a simple state (`master.git-dir`) to create our Git directory.

Then we can simply run this state and our master will be ready for us:

```
[vagrant@master srv]$ sudo salt master.example state.sls master.git-dir
master.example:
    ----------
<snip>

            ----------
        /srv/git:
            New Dir
<snip>
```

Then we need to create our Git repository (aka repo):

```
[vagrant@master srv]$ sudo git init /srv/git/salt-master.git
Initialized empty Git repository in /srv/git/salt-master.git/.git/
```

This will create a Git server at */srv/git/salt-master.git* and then populate it with a few files for demonstration purposes. Now, we need to configure the Salt master to use this new repo:

```
gitfs_remotes:
  - git://git@localhost:/srv/git/salt-master.git
```

As you can see, we simply add the Git URI to the `gitfs_remotes` configuration option. Earlier, we mentioned that the environments map to Git branches. This is simple enough—except in the case of the default branch and environment. In the Git world, the default branch is often named *master*. However, the default environment for Salt is usually named *base*. The `base` option used when we set up our Git directory means we will map the base environment to the *base* branch, not *master*. Remember, that option changes the name of the Git branch that maps to base, not the other way around.

Now we can see the results of the previous code by simply looking at the documentation for the modules. But remember, since this is a new change, we have to either restart the minions or sync:

```
$ sudo salt '*' saltutil.sync_all
```

Now we can look at the output of *sys.doc* to see the module that is available only via the preceding Git repo:

```
$ sudo salt master.example sys.doc git_test
```

Topology Variations

Throughout this book, we have been working with Salt using a simple, albeit standard, setup: a single master with multiple minions. Salt has several other options. The simplest of these is running the minions without any master. Next, there is a *peer system* whereby a special group of minions can execute commands via the master to a set of minions. Also, *syndication masters* will act as a proxy so that a subset of minions does not connect directly to the master, but is still controlled by it. Lastly, there is a way to have several masters, thereby removing the single point of failure.

Masterless Minions

The master allows for centralized control and management of your minions. Salt provides a wealth of functionality that is not directly related to the masters controlling the minions. The state system itself is a powerful way to enforce a specific configuration on a host. Running a state locally still provides that power. Also, the modules that ship with Salt, and those from third parties, provide a fantastic abstraction layer from which you can execute the same command on many different architectures.

The key to all this power is the salt-call command. We have discussed it in passing many times throughout this book. As you might recall, the salt-call command is just like the main salt command, but since it *always* runs against *localhost*, it does not have a target, or a list of minions:

```
[vagrant@minion1 ~]$ sudo salt-call test.ping
local:
    True
```

Let's stop the salt-master process and see what happens:

```
[vagrant@master ~]$ sudo service salt-master stop
Stopping salt-master daemon:                          [  OK  ]

[vagrant@minion1 ~]$ sudo salt-call test.ping
Attempt to authenticate with the salt master failed
```

When we use salt-call on the minion, it still expects to be able to communicate with the master. The communication with the master allows the minion to make sure its pillar data, as well as any files from the file server, is up to date. We can skip that step by adding the --local flag:

```
[vagrant@minion1 ~]$ sudo salt-call --local test.ping
local:
    True
```

This is fine for single events, but if this is the layout you desire, then we should configure the minion to not communicate with the master.

Typing in the --local flag every time would be a pain. Let's add a configuration option to the minion so that it always assumes that it is running without a master. Since the minion no longer needs to communicate with a master, there does not need to be a daemon running to maintain the communication channel. The salt-call command will read the configuration and execute commands as needed:

```
[vagrant@minion1 ~]$ sudo service salt-minion stop
Stopping salt-minion daemon:                          [  OK  ]
[vagrant@minion1 ~]$ cat /etc/salt/minion.d/masterless.conf
file_client: local
[vagrant@minion1 ~]$ sudo salt-call --local test.ping
local:
    True
```

Since the minion will no longer communicate with a master, it must know where to look for data that is normally retrieved via the file server. We can use the same setup we use on the master, but this time in the minion's configuration:

```
[vagrant@minion1 ~]$ cat /etc/salt/minion.d/masterless.conf
file_client: local

file_roots:
  base:
  - /srv/salt/local/file/base
```

Next, just as with the master, we will need a *top.sls* file so that Salt will know what states are in the highstate. Also, let's create a very simple Salt state on the local filesystem so we can verify that everything looks good:

```
[vagrant@minion1 ~]$ cat /srv/salt/local/file/base/top.sls
base:
  '*':
    - mytest
[vagrant@minion1 ~]$ cat /srv/salt/local/file/base/mytest.sls
mytest:
  test.succeed_with_changes:
  - name: foo
```

Now, we can view the top file and then run a highstate:

```
[vagrant@minion1 ~]$ sudo salt-call --log-level=warning state.show_top
local:
    ----------
    base:
        - mytest
[vagrant@minion1 ~]$ sudo salt-call --log-level=warning state.highstate
local:
  ----------
          ID: mytest
    Function: test.succeed_with_changes
        Name: foo
      Result: True
     Comment: Success!
     Started: 04:37:57.477314
    Duration: 0.681 ms
     Changes:
                  ----------
                  testing:
                      ----------
                      new:
                          Something pretended to change
                      old:
                          Unchanged

Summary
----------
Succeeded: 1 (changed=1)
Failed:    0
----------
Total states run:     1
```

When this is combined with the various software configuration management (SCM)-backed file stores (e.g., `gitfs`), you can create a system that is entirely standalone, yet provides many of the features that make up the core of Salt.

Peer System

Having a centralized master makes it very easy for a small group to manage a great many systems. And the ACL system can provide a way for others to log in to the master and run a small set of commands. But giving others access to that main host does present some security challenges. The peer system provides a way for select minions to send commands through the master to other minions. The list of commands can also be limited.

Publishers

The first step is configuring the master with the list of minions and the list of commands they can run. We will use a very simple case of a single minion (`minion1`) to be able to run all of the commands in the `test` module:

```
[vagrant@master ~]$ sudo cat /etc/salt/master.d/peer.conf
peer:
  minion1.example:
  - test.*
```

Now we should be able to run the command from the peer, `minion1`. Remember that the minions do not have the `salt` command; however, they do have the `salt-call` command. There is a module specifically for peer communication: `publish`. Keep in mind that all we are essentially doing is publishing a command onto the `publish` port of the pub-sub system. (Also, we need to listen for return data on that same system.)

```
[vagrant@minion1 ~]$ sudo salt-call publish.publish \* test.ping
[INFO    ] Publishing 'test.ping' to tcp://172.31.0.11:4506
local:
    ----------
    master.example:
        True
    minion1.example:
        True
    minion2.example:
        True
    minion3.example:
        True
    minion4.example:
        True
```

Runners

The `publish.publish` command simply takes as arguments a target (for which minions should run a command) and then the command itself. But you can also execute runners from the master using the `publish.runner` command. As with the `salt-run` command, there is no targeting information given.

We need to again configure the master to specify which minions can execute which runner commands:

```
[vagrant@master ~]$ cat /etc/salt/master.d/peer.conf
peer:
  minion1.example:
  - test.*
peer_run:
  minion1.example:
  - jobs.*
```

Now we can run any jobs runners from `minion1`:

```
[vagrant@minion1 ~]$ sudo salt-call publish.runner jobs.list_jobs
[INFO    ] Publishing runner 'jobs.list_jobs' to tcp://172.31.0.11:4506
local:
    ----------
    20150111230518279413:
        ----------
        Arguments:
        Function:
            test.ping
        StartTime:
            2015, Jan 11 23:05:18.279413
        Target:
            minion1.example
        Target-type:
            glob
        User:
            root
<snip>
```

Remember that the minion that has access to the peer system simply has access to the master—nothing else. In the case of execution modules, the modules still run on each minion and then return data to the master. And with runners, the Python code executes on the master, not on the peer.

The peer system provides a great deal of flexibility, but it does open up some security concerns. You need to treat any minions with such rights as "special."

Syndication Masters

With the peer system, a minion can run a command, but it still needs to go through the master. This means that all minions will still need a connection to the master on both the publish and return ports. There are situations where this may become a problem—for example, if you have a significant number of minions and the sheer volume of TCP (transmission control protocol) connections is too much, or if you have a geographically dispersed network and you still need a centralized master. This is where the *syndication master* comes into play. The syndication master looks like a minion to the "master of masters," but looks like a master to the minions attached to it. It simply forwards commands down to its minions and then also relays return information from the minions back to its master.

With our relatively small setup, it is difficult to simulate a variety of topologies. We will show a very basic setup where `minion1` is a syndication master (`syndic`) and `minion2` is attached to it.

First, we need to set up the `syndic` master on `minion1`. We can leverage Salt's `pkg` module:

```
[vagrant@minion1 ~]$ sudo salt-call pkg.install salt-syndic
<snip>
```

Next, we need to configure the `syndic` running on `minion1`:

```
[vagrant@minion1 ~]$ cat /etc/salt/master/syndic.conf
syndic_master: 172.31.0.11
syndic_master_port: 4506
syndic_log_file: /var/log/salt/syndic.log
syndic_pidfile: /var/run/salt-syndic.pid
```

Now just start the `salt-syndic` service:

```
[vagrant@minion1 ~]$ sudo service salt-syndic start
Starting salt-syndic daemon:                         [  OK  ]
```

We also need to change the minion configuration on both `minion2` and `minion1` to communicate with the `syndic`, not the main master:

```
[vagrant@minion1 ~]$ cat /etc/salt/minion.d/99-master-address.conf
master: 172.31.0.21
[vagrant@minion2 ~]$ cat /etc/salt/minion.d/99-master-address.conf
master: 172.31.0.21
```

(Obviously, you will need to restart the `salt-minion` daemon on each host as well.)

 Since the syndication master is, essentially, a Salt master for all minions connected to it, the `syndic` needs to track the public keys of those minions. It also needs a *file_roots* directory, *pillar_roots* directory, and so on.

Multiple Masters

The previous solutions provide several ways of working with different topologies. However, when running a master with directly attached minions, we still face the problem of a single point of failure. You can run multiple masters if this is a concern.

There are a number of considerations when you are running multiple masters against a set of minions, though.

Since each minion can only have a single master key, all of your masters in that cluster must have the same key pair.

Next, the minions will return data only to the master that sent the command. Thus, if you have two masters where each one is "equal," then you will need to check both for return data. You *can* share the job cache between all masters using, say, an NFS (Network File System) server. However, this further complicates the maintenance and setup.

Also, remember that the master checks that a command sent to a minion does not interfere with a command that is still in progress. With multiple masters, this data would not be shared between them. As a result you may get into a very nasty situation of deadlock, where one master is trying to perform a command that the other master is actively trying to revert.

Since both masters will be sending data (via the file server and pillar roots) to each minion, you will need to keep all of those files in sync on every master.

Lastly, all minions will need to talk to all masters on both the publish and return ports. This can be a significant amount of network connections and/or traffic.

Another possibility with multiple masters is to have a master for a specific purpose. For example, if you have a number of regularly scheduled jobs that run through Salt, you may consider running the scheduled jobs on one master and leave the other master for interactive jobs. If you break up the files involved and the states/modules, you can even minimize the possibility of the deadlock just mentioned. However, this does not give you a real *high-availability* solution; it simply spreads the load onto multiple hosts. If your master is greatly overburdened, though, this may be an option for you.

 While working at a very large company with tens of thousands of minions, we never ran multiple masters for a given set of minions. We did have an additional host as a *warm standby*, just in case. But we never had to use it. There is continued work around a true high-availability setup, but it has not been completed at the time of this writing.

Running multiple masters may work in certain situations, but it is not something you should do haphazardly. Consider the aforementioned issues and weigh them carefully against the problem you are trying to solve. As with the rest of Salt, this area is evolving and maturing every day. Having a true high-availability solution is of interest to many people.

CHAPTER 10

Brief Introduction to salt-cloud

Overview

This entire book has used examples running on virtualized systems. But the setup and install of those systems was a bit manual. More and more companies are using virtual machines to quickly introduce new applications and to expand existing ones. Hopefully, the advantages of virtual machines are evident. As powerful as they are, though, virtual machines still require an operating system to be installed and managed. This is where salt-cloud can help. It provides an abstraction layer that makes interacting with the different vendors easier.

There are several very large vendors that provide cloud services and a number of smaller ones. Amazon is one of the leaders in cloud services, offering a number of different services above and beyond basic virtual machines. In order to keep this chapter focused on the basics, we are going to focus on Amazon's service, Amazon Web Services (AWS). The salt-cloud documentation (*http://bit.ly/salt_docs*) has examples for many other providers.

We are going to assume some basic familiarity with AWS. There are numerous sites that can help you get started quickly. A simple web search (*http://bit.ly/ aws_get_started*) should provide you with plenty of options to get your feet wet.

Setup: AWS and salt-cloud

The first thing we need to do is create a user specific to our new infrastructure. While using your existing credentials will work, it is advised that you keep your primary credentials to yourself. If you, for example, happen to check in your keys accidentally, you will want to easily delete that user and add a new one.

Create a user named se-book-demo via the IAM (Identity and Access Management) user management console. You will need to copy the credentials right after you create the user. Next, you will need to attach a policy with administrator access.

Now that you have a user created, you will need to create a key pair so you can access any new instances created. In the main EC2 console, select Key Pairs and create a new pair. We need to put this key somewhere Salt can access it. Copy the key to your current master and place it in the root home directory. The permissions need to be pretty restrictive, so change them as follows just to prevent any problems later:

```
[vagrant@master ~]$ sudo chmod 400 /root/se-book-key.pem
[vagrant@master ~]$ sudo ls -l /root/se-book-key.pem
-r--------. 1 root root 1692 Mar  1 23:22 /root/se-book-key.pem
```

At this point, we have the necessary information from Amazon to get started. Remember that the minions need to connect to the master, not the other way around. Since our current Salt master is running on our local system, we need to create a master in AWS that the minions can use. Fortunately, Salt can help us with that. We will need to install salt-cloud on our current Salt master.

Installing salt-cloud

In the past, the salt-cloud code was stored in a different repo from the Salt core. Today, salt-cloud has been rolled into the Salt core, but there is still a different package for salt-cloud. Rather than installing the package directly, we should continue to use Salt to make sure our master is in the state we desire.

We can expand on our earlier use of the *master* state file. Add a new entry specifically for setting up salt-cloud:

```
[vagrant@master ~]$ cat /srv/salt/file/base/master/init.sls
include:
- .peer-setup
- .cloud-setup

[vagrant@master ~]$ cat /srv/salt/file/base/master/cloud-setup.sls
master_cloud_setup_packages:
  pkg.installed:
  - pkgs:
    - salt-cloud
[vagrant@master ~]$ sudo salt master.example state.sls master.cloud-setup
<snip>
```

This will add the necessary binaries and create the base directories that we will use to bootstrap our AWS infrastructure.

Before we actually create the Salt master, we need to set up a couple of Salt's configuration files. The *cloud providers* configuration lists the details of the hosting provider. Next is the *cloud profiles*, which will list how we want individual instances configured.

Cloud Providers

As we mentioned, Salt can interact with a number of different vendors that provide virtualization services. They all have slight differences in general credential management and a host of other properties. The cloud providers configuration will allow us to encapsulate that information for various vendors. But even within a single vendor like AWS, there may be different options at a very high level. A great example is the different regions that AWS supports. You can define a different *provider* for each region. Or, maybe, you have different subaccounts that link back to a main account. Or, you may have different security groups within the same account. Many of these different, high-level settings can be grouped together in the providers configuration. We are going to use a very simple example.

As we saw in the configuration of the Salt master, you can either edit a single, large file or create multiple smaller files in a configuration directory. We are going to opt for the latter. So, let's create a simple file for AWS:

```
[vagrant@master ~]$ cat /etc/salt/cloud.providers.d/aws.conf
se-book-aws:
  id: [AWS_ACCESS_KEY]
  key: [AWS_SECRET_KEY]
  keyname: se-book-key
  securitygroup: default
  private_key: /root/se-book-key.pem
  provider: ec2
```

In place of the `id` and `key` values, you would use the values of the AWS access and secret keys generated when you created the user named `se-book-user`. The key pair file should be located at */root/se-book-key.pem*, as we showed in the previous section. The security group is simply set to `default`. This is a setting within AWS itself. Feel free to use any security group that you have set up. We will use the simplest case, the `default` group, to keep ourselves from getting bogged down in the huge number of options that AWS provides. The last line, `provider: ec2`, will direct `salt-cloud` as to which set of modules to use when managing our instances. This line needs to come from the list of providers known to `salt-cloud`. We can verify using the `--list-providers` argument to `salt-cloud`:

```
[vagrant@master ~]$ sudo salt-cloud --list-providers
[INFO    ] salt-cloud starting
se-book-aws:
    ----------
    ec2:
        ----------
```

As you can see, the key we created, se-book-aws, is present. While this simple case doesn't tell us much, once you start adding providers, this command is a good place to go if you are having configuration problems.

Now that salt-cloud knows some additional details about the provider, we need to tell it more information about the instances we want to create. For this, we will need to configure the cloud profiles.

Cloud Profiles

After the cloud provider is configured, we need to define how we want the specific instances configured:

```
[vagrant@master ~]$ cat /etc/salt/cloud.profiles.d/se-book.conf
se-book-basic:
  provider: se-book-aws
  image: ami-8e682ce6
  size: t1.micro
  ssh_username: ec2-user
  securitygroup:
  - default
```

This should all look pretty familiar if you have worked with AWS before. The pro vider key is a reference to the provider we just created. An image is an operating system base image; this particular image is a generic Amazon Linux install. The image is important for the default user specified with ssh_username. This user, combined with the key pair defined in the provider, will allow Salt to connect and get the host prepped for Salt use. The size uses AWS-specific terms and gives the amount of CPU, RAM, and a few other system parameters.

At this point we could create the image using salt-cloud. However, given that our current master is a virtual machine on your local system, the new hosts won't be able to communicate with our current master. (You could definitely configure your firewall to talk to your current master, if you wish. But that is well beyond the scope of this book.) We need to create a master using the make_master declaration inside a *cloud map file*. The cloud map will connect the preceding profile with hostnames and any additional configuration settings.

Cloud Maps

The cloud map is very straightforward. It simply maps any of the profiles defined to a list of hosts. All we want to do for the moment is create a new Salt master, so we only need a single entry:

```
[vagrant@master ~]$ cat /etc/salt/cloud.maps.d/se-book.conf
se-book-basic:
  - host0:
    make_master: True
```

We just start out with a key with the name of a valid profile: se-book-basic. Then we simply list the hostnames with any additional configuration defined. In this case, we are adding the make_master key to our first host so we can get our infrastructure started. We then just call salt-cloud to get our first host set up:

```
[vagrant@master ~]$ sudo salt-cloud -m /etc/salt/cloud.maps.d/se-book.conf
[INFO    ] salt-cloud starting
[INFO    ] Applying map from '/etc/salt/cloud.maps.d/se-book.conf'.
The following virtual machines are set to be created:
  host0

Proceed? [N/y] y
... proceeding
[INFO    ] Calculating dependencies for host0
<snip>
```

Now we can log in using the username defined previously and our key pair:

```
local-system$ ssh -i .ssh/se-book-key.pem \
    ec2-user@ec2-private-ip-addr.compute-1.amazonaws.com
```

Introspection via salt-cloud

After you have logged in to your new master, you will need to copy over the various cloud settings files:

```
/etc/salt/cloud.providers.d/aws.conf
/etc/salt/cloud.profiles.d/se-book.conf
/etc/salt/cloud.maps.d/se-book.conf
/root/se-book-key.pem
```

 Remember to update the permissions on the private key file: /root/ se-book-key.pem.

The salt-cloud command has a few options to give you a better look into your cloud infrastructure and what is available. We already saw the --list-providers option:

```
[ec2-user@private-ip-addr ~]$ sudo salt-cloud --list-providers
se-book-aws:
    ----------
    ec2:
        ----------
```

We can also look at the images available using --list-images. You need to supply the provider name as an argument. The list of images is very large. You can narrow it down by adding an owner key to your provider configuration.

AWS has several data centers throughout the world. You can query the available locations using `--list-locations`. Again, it takes as an argument the provider ID. (Remember, the provider configuration includes the AWS access and secret keys, which are used to communicate with the various AWS data stores.)

```
[ec2-user@private-ip-addr ~]$ sudo salt-cloud --list-locations se-book-aws
se-book-aws:
    ----------
    ec2:
        ----------
<snip>
        us-east-1:
            ----------
            endpoint:
                ec2.us-east-1.amazonaws.com
            name:
                us-east-1
<snip>
```

Lastly, AWS has many options for the size of machine you can provision. No surprise: `salt-cloud` includes the `--list-sizes` flag:

```
[ec2-user@private-ip-addr ~]$ sudo salt-cloud --list-sizes se-book-aws
se-book-aws:
    ----------
    ec2:
        ----------
<snip>
        Micro:
            ----------
            t1.micro:
                ----------
                cores:
                    1
                disk:
                    EBS
                id:
                    t1.micro
                ram:
                    615 MiB
        Standard:
            ----------
            m1.large:
<snip>
```

That list is also very large. The details aren't that important, but it *is* important to know there is more in `salt-cloud` than just creating instances; you can also query the provider and gain some insight into what they provide. However, this functionality varies widely among the different cloud providers. Be sure to verify that any specific function you need is actually supported by your given vendor.

So far we have created only our single master. We are going to finish up with some simple examples of how you can manage an entire infrastructure using salt-cloud.

Creating an Infrastructure

Let's get right to it and add another host. Earlier we showed you the *map file* when we created the master. We simply want to add another host to that list. However, we also want to customize the information about that host just a little:

```
[ec2-user@private-ip-addr ~]$ cat /etc/salt/cloud.maps.d/se-book.conf
se-book-basic:
  - host0:
      make_master: True
  - host1:
      grains:
        role: test
        myenv: prod
```

We added a host named host1 and configured it with a couple of familiar grains. One of the first things you'll notice is that we do not have to accept the key of the minions we add. salt-cloud will automatically add any new hosts it configures to the known list of keys:

```
[ec2-user@private-ip-addr ~]$ sudo salt-key
Accepted Keys:
host1
Unaccepted Keys:
Rejected Keys:
```

We will add just one more host to show how you can add further minion settings in the map file:

```
[ec2-user@private-ip-addr ~]$ cat /etc/salt/cloud.maps.d/se-book.conf
se-book-basic:
  - host0:
      make_master: True
  - host1:
      grains:
        role: test
        myenv: prod
  - host2:
      minion:
        log_level: debug
      grains:
        role: test
        myenv: dev
```

While it may not be very exciting to just enable debug logging on our third host, it gives you an indication of what can be done. Most minion settings are available via the map file. This will allow you to control your new infrastructure right from the creation of your instances.

More Information

We have only scratched the surface of what you can do with salt-cloud. There are over a dozen different providers supported with the basic installation. And as with the rest of Salt, you can create your own provider. But there is a caveat here: the data and functionality provided will vary greatly from vendor to vendor. Salt does its best to abstract out the details and provide a common interface to all of its supported vendors. But sometimes the data or function needed simply isn't there. As a result, the capabilities of salt-cloud are strongly linked to the vendor you choose. Also, since Salt is a large open source community, the larger vendors will simply have better support due to the large percentage of Salt users using them. It should not come as a surprise that we chose AWS for the examples in this chapter. It is heavily used throughout the industry, so there are a lot of people pairing salt-cloud with AWS because it's a more thoroughly tested provider.

Providers change their APIs and update their infrastructure. salt-cloud has to keep up with all of these changes. But don't view this as a problem; rather, it is an opportunity for you to contribute to a growing community.

Using Vagrant to Run Salt Examples

There are many options for setting up a suite of minions to use in the examples. Vagrant (*https://www.vagrantup.com/*) is a great solution that runs on top of a free virtual machine manager called *VirtualBox* (*https://www.virtualbox.org/*).

There is a Git repo at GitHub (*https://github.com/craig5/salt-essentials-utils*) that contains the companion code for this book.

Install Companion Code, VirtualBox, and Vagrant

To get started, simply clone the repo to your local machine:

```
git clone https://github.com/craig5/salt-essentials-utils
```

You will also need to install Vagrant and VirtualBox using the instructions on their respective websites.

Once you have all three pieces ready, you can start up the virtual machines used in the examples with:

```
host$ cd salt-essentials-utils/virtual-machines/
host$ vagrant up
```

This will download the base images and create a master running CentOS 6.6, two minions also running CentOS 6.6, and two more minions running Ubuntu Trusty Tahr (14.04).

The virtual machines do require unused memory if you do not want to degrade the performance of your host machine. Each node will use 512 MB of RAM. If you are not able to spare that much memory, consider running only a single minion of each OS type. You will have to modify the example accordingly.

Configure Salt

Once you have the virtual machines set up, you will need to install Salt on each one. Fortunately, the example code is made available to each host via a special mount: */srv/se-book*. There is a *setup* script in the *bin* directory that will configure each host:

```
[vagrant@minion1 ~]$ sudo /srv/se-book/bin/setup
```

The Salt packages are downloaded via the *bootstrap* script mentioned in Chapter 2. The shared code packages are installed, as well as the salt-minion. For the virtual machine named master.example, the salt-master package is also installed. The necessary daemons are then started. At this point, you should have the minions ready to go to proceed to "Key Management" on page 19 and accept all of the keys.

 The *bootstrap* script is meant to be an easy way to get a demo version set up. The underlying command is not 100 percent secure. While it uses a reliable server to download the script, it does so using an insecure channel. If you are concerned about security in the slightest, please install Salt using the instructions on Salt's website. This *only* affects the install of Salt, not the setup of the virtual machines themselves.

YAML

YAML stands for *YAML Ain't Markup Language*. (It used to be something else, but was changed to focus more on its data-oriented nature.) YAML is used heavily throughout Salt; from state files (SLS) to all of the configuration files, you will find YAML in many places. We have assumed that you have some basic familiarity with YAML and can thus follow along with the simple use cases in this book.

In order to better visualize the following example, we will use an online YAML parser (*http://yaml-online-parser.appspot.com/*). You can enter YAML in one text box and see a JSON representation next to it.

However, as with any language, YAML does have some quirks. Just like Python, YAML uses indentation for scoping, but you have to use spaces and not tabs. If you are having difficulty with states not compiling properly or with configuration files not being read as you expect, first make sure you do not have your editor set to replace spaces with tabs.

The next thing you should know is that YAML uses a leading hash (#) as an indicator for a comment. This is just like many scripting languages. For example, bash, Perl, and Python all use the hash for comments.

YAML has data structures for strings, integers, lists (arrays), and dictionaries. There are even shorthand ways of creating some of them. The data structures are formed using simple a *key*: *value* format.

While strings may be simple enough to understand, multiline strings have a couple of options. If you add a *greater than* sign (>), the end-of-line characters are removed:

```
mystring: >
  first line
  second line
  third line
```

```
{
    "mystring": "first line second line third line"
}
```

But if you replace that with a vertical pipe (|), then the end-of-line characters are pre-served:

```
mystring: |
  first line
  second line
  third line

{
    "mystring": "first line\nsecond line\nthird line"
}
```

Lists can be specified on separate lines with a leading dash:

```
list:
- first
- second
- third

{
    "list": [
      "first",
      "second",
      "third"
    ]
}
```

Or you can express them using a compact form that looks very similar to Python utilizing braces ([,]):

```
list: [first, second, third]

{
    "list": [
      "first",
      "second",
      "third"
    ]
}
```

Likewise, dictionaries have a longer and shorter format. Keys in a dictionary are indented below their parent:

```
dict:
  first: one
  second: two
  third: three

{
    "dict": {
      "second": "two",
      "third": "three",
```

```
    "first": "one"
  }
}
```

Here's the compact form, again similar to Python:

```
dict: {first: one, second: two, third: three}
{
  "dict": {
    "second": "two",
    "third": "three",
    "first": "one"
  }
}
```

YAML will also attempt to preserve integers as numeric data and not simply translate them into strings. So a value of 123 will not be a string, but an integer.

YAML does not require a value with every key. If a key exists by itself, a null value will be used. (In the case of Salt, this corresponds to a value of None.)

A couple of other features of YAML that we did not use in this book are anchors and references. Anchors are marked with an ampersand (&) and then can be referenced with an asterisk (*):

```
my_anchor: &mine bar
my_ref: *mine

{
  "my_anchor": "bar",
  "my_ref": "bar"
}
```

We define the key my_anchor, but we define the anchor itself with the name mine. It's important to note that the key does not play into the anchor at all. You can use the same name for the anchor as the key, or not. In the next key, my_ref, we reference the mine anchor using an asterisk. This allows us to define a value once, but use it many times in the same file.

This is only a quick introduction to YAML. You can find the complete specification on the YAML website (*http://www.yaml.org/*).

Next, we will mention some specifics about YAML and Salt.

One of the main things to keep in mind is that Salt uses the PyYAML library for parsing all of its YAML files. PyYAML has many handy features. If there is a value that seems to be a date-time, it will convert it into a datetime object. For example:

```
2015-03-02 07:06:15
```

PyYAML will interpret several different strings to be Boolean values—for example, yes/no, true/false, TRUE/FALSE.

If you use UTF-8 in your state files, you should enable the `yaml_utf8` setting in your master's configuration. This will enable additional routines to parse UTF-8 strings.

Lastly, Salt recommends using two spaces for indentation in your YAML files. Obviously, you can use any spacing you prefer, as long as you are consistent in each file. But once you start to share files with others, any inconsistencies will be a little jarring.

Index

About the Authors

Craig Sebenik was responsible for the Salt infrastructure while at LinkedIn. LinkedIn is still one of the largest deployments of Salt in the world today. He is now at a startup, Matterport (*http://matterport.com/*), using Salt in the cloud and with a small team of developers. Working in companies both large and small has given him rare insight into the use of Salt, and being involved since version 0.8 has given Craig a front-row seat for the evolution of Salt through the years.

Thomas Hatch is the creator of Salt and CTO of SaltStack. Thomas is still the largest contributor to the Salt project despite the fact that Salt is now the largest developer community in DevOps.

Colophon

The animal on the cover of *Salt Essentials* is a conger eel, found in ocean waters around the world. Several species of eel belong to the genus *Conger*, including the European conger, which can grow to almost 10 feet and weigh more than any other species of eel on the planet.

Details about the conger eel's lifecycle are not abundant, but both the European and American conger eels appear to exhibit the reproductive behaviors common to other kinds of eel. For instance, they both seem to take as many as 15 years to reach sexual maturity, when they travel to deeper waters to spawn. Females produce eggs in the millions and, according to popular conception, die immediately after spawning. Conger eel larvae drift from deeper to shallower waters over a period of up to two years after hatching. They complete this journey as *leptocephali*, that is, as transparent, laterally compressed fish in the process of metamorphosing into mature eels.

Mature congers pass days in the crevices and holes of rocky ocean landscapes or among the rotting remains of shipwrecks and can venture out as predators at night. They hunt smaller fish and crustaceans but are not above scavenging the ocean floor for dead or dying fish. They have been known to attack humans.

Many of the animals on O'Reilly covers are endangered; all of them are important to the world. To learn more about how you can help, go to *animals.oreilly.com*.

The cover image is from Johnson's *Natural History*. The cover fonts are URW Typewriter and Guardian Sans. The text font is Adobe Minion Pro; the heading font is Adobe Myriad Condensed; and the code font is Dalton Maag's Ubuntu Mono.

Get even more for your money.

Join the O'Reilly Community, and register the O'Reilly books you own. It's free, and you'll get:

- $4.99 ebook upgrade offer
- 40% upgrade offer on O'Reilly print books
- Membership discounts on books and events
- Free lifetime updates to ebooks and videos
- Multiple ebook formats, DRM FREE
- Participation in the O'Reilly community
- Newsletters
- Account management
- 100% Satisfaction Guarantee

Signing up is easy:

1. Go to: oreilly.com/go/register
2. Create an O'Reilly login.
3. Provide your address.
4. Register your books.

Note: English-language books only

To order books online:
oreilly.com/store

For questions about products or an order:
orders@oreilly.com

To sign up to get topic-specific email announcements and/or news about upcoming books, conferences, special offers, and new technologies:
elists@oreilly.com

For technical questions about book content:
booktech@oreilly.com

To submit new book proposals to our editors:
proposals@oreilly.com

O'Reilly books are available in multiple DRM-free ebook formats. For more information:
oreilly.com/ebooks

O'REILLY®

CPSIA information can be obtained at www.ICGtesting.com
Printed in the USA
LVOW03s2229280715

448033LV00010B/37/P

9 781491 900635